CREATE IN ME
A YOUTH
MINISTRY

Create in me

A YOUTH MINISTRY

RIDGE BURNS
with Pam Campbell

VICTOR BOOKS™

A DIVISION OF SCRIPTURE PRESS PUBLICATIONS INC.
USA CANADA ENGLAND

Scripture quotations are from the *Holy Bible,
New International Version,* © 1973, 1978, 1984,
International Bible Society. Used by permis-
sion of Zondervan Bible Publishers.

Library of Congress Catalog Card Number:
86-60877

ISBN: 0-89693-636-8

This book is dedicated to Robanne, my best friend and wife, and my son, R.W., whose smile causes me to work harder to make his future brighter by helping high school students change their world today.

Ridge Burns

This book is dedicated to Stan, my partner in marriage and youth ministry, and my "kids" at Lisle Bible Church.

Pam Campbell

Some names in this book have been changed to protect confidentiality.

CONTENTS

FOREWORD

I don't know how it felt for you, but my first year was the hardest.

Inter-Varsity Christian Fellowship had assigned me to pioneer a campus ministry at a large, two-year community college. Like most young, zealous youth worker types, I wanted to make history for God. And like most young, zealous youth worker types, I believed the key to making that history was developing the best techniques. If I could concoct fantastic programs, brainstorm creative ideas, and formulate ingenious motivational strategies . . . then God could begin to move.

Ministering at a "commuter" college meant that I quickly got in touch with the area churches whose kids fed into my school. That of course put me in touch with the youth pastors at these churches. They turned out to be a lot like me—young, zealous youth worker types who wanted to make their own kind of history for God. They were sincere, highly motivated, and committed to the Lord and His kingdom ministry.

But I digress. What made my first year so hard? I could tell you it was because the ministry floundered, but in fact the Inter-Varsity work on my campus exceeded the organization's highest hopes. I could tell you it was because the area churches weren't enthusiastic about my parachurch presence, but in fact they welcomed me with open arms and open budgets. I could tell you it was because the youth pastors I got to know were a sour, motley bunch, but in fact they were a wonderful group of godly men and women.

No . . . my first year was so hard because I felt so alone. Although I'd been supplied with an impressive array of books and other resources designed to help me plan, strategize, manage, and implement my ministry program, I could find nothing to help me work through the bewildering mosaic of feelings I was experiencing. Why did I feel so out of my depth? Why did most of the preparatory material that I read become irrelevant the minute I stepped on campus? Did other youth workers feel as threatened as I did when I received criticism? I'd felt so qualified for youth ministry; how was I to cope with the bewilderment I felt as a student poured out his struggles with his homosexual tendencies?

I remember scouring the Christian bookstores in my area, frantically searching for something on youth ministry that dealt on a level other than program, management, or philosophy. No luck. *Who knows*, I thought. *Maybe I'm abnormal or something, and no one else feels this way.*

Fortunately, I wasn't as abnormal as I feared. As my friendships with my fellow youth workers (including the author of this book) deepened, we slowly began to share not only our programs, but our feelings—and discovered to our mutual delight that we had much in common.

How refreshing it was to find that I wasn't the only one who found real-life youth ministry to be radically different than what I'd been taught to expect; to realize that criticism made others feel defensive as it did me; to know that my associates were as clueless as I was as to just what "normal" youth ministry was.

The fellowship and sharing I enjoyed with those youth workers had much to do with getting me through those traumatic early years. But I know too many youth workers who, lacking the good fortune of this kind of peer support, buckled under the pressure of their aloneness and found another line of work.

That's why I'm so delighted that Ridge Burns has decided to open his personal journey to us in this book. Finally, a youth pastor who has paid his dues (and developed some fantastic youth ministries) shares from his heart, and his gut, how it felt to live through formative years of his work, and his life. I've had the privilege of knowing Ridge as an associate and as a friend for the last eight years. Now you will be able to get to know him.

And get to know him you will. One thing I like about Ridge is that he doesn't pull any punches. It's a well-worn saying, but "tells it like it is" applies to Ridge as well as to anyone I know. This book reflects his fresh, straightforward approach to life and ministry. You'll find no artificial, make-believe sweet talk here. You'll relive his ups, downs, joys, sorrows; his thoughts and feelings as he travels his journey. If you're like me, you'll find yourself laughing, crying, wincing, and even nodding your head emphatically as you say to yourself, "Yeah! I've felt that way!" It's that kind of book.

Best of all, it's not just an interesting story. Ridge Burns is a man who has served his Lord. Through Project Serve, Sidewalk Sunday School, and his day-in, day-out caring for high school kids, he *is* making history for God. I consider him the E.F. Hutton of youth ministry: when he talks, the rest of us would be wise to listen.

And it's his wisdom, forged over more than a decade of ministry, that makes this book so valuable. What Ridge has discovered through his years of service is that it's what's inside a person that makes the ministry, not the other way around. All the dazzling techniques in the world are meaningless if our hearts and souls are not first fueled by the fire of the Holy Spirit and the desire to fulfill His agenda for the young people entrusted to us. The exciting part is that when we do open ourselves to the power and guidance of our Lord—including His gentle, loving work in us as we struggle with our own feelings and emotions—real gospel history will be made, through people like you and me.

That's the encouragement I found in this book; I trust that you will find it too. Enjoy!

Noel Becchetti, Editor
Youthworker

PASTORS' LETTERS

I

There he sat, draped over the restaurant chair. Unlike others I had interviewed for the staff job, his appearance was a step-and-a-half under casual. No nerves surfaced undisguised for me to freely see. It was a little intimidating for a pastor who made sure he was ready so that this about-to-be-graduated seminary student would know that it was a privilege to be interviewed by me.

Now that I look back on it, we hardly talked about "Your call to the ministry, Ridge?" or "How would you handle it if . . . ?" But why should we have talked about such things? Here, obvious to anyone who could get past his gangly legs hung over the corner of the breakfast table, was a success story about to be written, six-and-a-half feet of untamed energy in search of a church, an encyclopedia of ideas about to be read into some people's lives. I liked him immediately.

Ridge's journal tells the rest of the story. Sometimes strikeouts and sometimes home runs. Creating. Toughening. Softening. Growing. Waiting. Down. Up. Ahead of his time and behind in his paperwork. With tough skin and marshmallow center. Fiercely loyal. Slightly irreverent. Genuinely Ridge.

As I watched Ridge make his journey into the best youth ministry I had yet to see, I could readily see that his heart was set on the spiritual growth of those he served, his character always authentically Christian, and his willingness to give of himself, extravagant. As senior pastor, there were times to say, "Sit on it, Ridge!" and at other times, "Go for it." There were times for me to lead, but many times for me to follow.

The youth ministry of the church we served together grew from a dozen to 10 dozen. The Flock, the Fish Factory, the Carpenter's Union, Mexicali, Servant Day, Junior High Superstars, and more—all born out of the pains of Ridge's first ministry—became as much a part of the Walnut Creek Church as hymns on Sunday and prayers on Wednesday. If the value of a man's past work is to be found in what happens after he leaves, then the continuing strength of those ministries is a high tribute to Ridge Burns.

With mixed emotions, I accepted his resignation one day. It was an unhappy day for the Walnut Creek Church and me. But we were all aware that while it meant the setting of one day's sun for us, it was at the same time another sunrise for Ridge and Robanne and a future for them that would have an impact on youth ministries again and again. May God give His church more people like Ridge Burns.

Charles A. Wickman, Pastor
Bethany Church of Sierra Madre
Sierra Madre, California

II

There was enough energy in the atrium that afternoon to fuel the four Greyhound buses warming their engines outside in the church parking lot. One hundred and eighty high schoolers had packed their skis, sleeping bags, and suitcases (no radios!) into the luggage compartments. Now pictures were being taken, streamers thrown from the second level, horns blown, and balloons launched. It was snowing outside, but the atmosphere inside was that of a boat leaving on a Caribbean cruise.

Winter retreat was about to become a reality. I was watching it come together, all the things that I had read about in the minutes that were published over the months of planning: The "Love Boat" theme, the publicity committee, the committee on transportation, devotional guides, the speaker, the musicians, cabin assignments, and more. It was all so carefully planned and documented in two thick notebooks. And now the ship was about to sail.

Rev. Ridgeway W. Burns dominated the room with his enthusiasm. When Ridge has fun, everyone has fun. He had more energy than 10 of his high schoolers. And most of them were there not to attend an event but because of a relationship he had developed with them and they with him. Parents and church staff looked on with wonder. "Who is this number one high schooler? He's the biggest kid of the lot!"

Only those "in the know," who themselves are experienced professionals, realize what was happening. The spontaneity was carefully programmed. Only someone with the confidence of two thick notebooks could have the kind of freedom Ridge had in the atrium. It was all carefully laid out and planned. There was nothing to do but enjoy it to the fullest with the kids.

I have worked with a number of high school youth leaders through 30 years of ministry, and they are a special breed. Just as great preachers have an initial gift from God which must be fanned into flame, Ridge knows that this is what God has called him to do. He wants to be in youth ministry more than anything else he can imagine.

If I were called to youth ministry, I would read books such as this one, and I would study diligently in school. But, above all, I would get with someone like a Ridge Burns and I would work *for* him until I had earned the right to work *with* him. Then, when I went into my own ministry, I would telephone him long distance every week, and never in off hours. The business department might not be happy, but my senior pastor would love me because of the ministry I would have going with kids. And now it would be my turn to teach someone else how to do high school youth work.

What a joy these five years have been at Wheaton Bible Church. The fun of working with Ridge is that I know we are both learning from one another and we are challenging each other to follow Christ more faithfully—and he can find me from anywhere in the world by telephone . . . collect!

Christopher A. Lyons, Former Senior Pastor
Wheaton Bible Church
Wheaton, Illinois

INTRODUCTION

Who is in charge of *your* youth ministry?

This may sound like a silly question, but think about it for a moment. Are you always looking for the latest books and materials, checking the latest trends, trying out all the new ideas you can find? Most of us are. But is that *all* you do? Have you become dependent on other people's ideas, programs, projects, and curricula? In other words, how much of *you* goes into *your* youth group?

Ridge Burns thinks the heart of any youth ministry is created out of the youth worker's relationship with God, the members of Christ's body (especially the students and their families), and the extended world community. These relationships are priorities which in turn create better programming, management, and strategies in youth ministry. The best youth programs are the ones that are created by God in you.

I hadn't met Ridge Burns prior to working with him on this book. Ridge's experience is with mega-churches, large-scale programs, enviable budgets, and pastoral responsibilities. My youth experience, on the other hand, is with a small church, sometimes no budget, and part-time responsibilities as a lay worker. In *Create in Me a Youth Ministry*, Ridge is the content person and I am the writer. But the more I worked with Ridge, the more I saw my history in his background. And I discovered that Ridge is a multileveled individual, which you will also find out as you read through this book.

On your first reading, Ridge may appear to be merely a storyteller. His first-person account of past failures and successes as a youth pastor is captivating. Through his journals (which he has

15

kept for the past 10 years), you will become aware of Ridge's philosophy of ministry and how his "created in me" ministry evolved.

Beneath the storyteller is an analyst. A closer examination of these chapters will reveal more than a collection of stories. Successes and failures are both of benefit if we learn from them. Ridge has analyzed these events of his past and interpreted each one as a learning experience. In the Small Church Spotlight sections of each chapter, Ridge has challenged me and helped me apply his principles for creating a youth ministry in my own small church setting.

Underneath everything else, Ridge is a vulnerable servant. I laughed at his ineptitude, because I've been there and am still making the same mistakes. I cried as I saw Ridge's "marshmallow center" and his deep hurt when he was criticized for being ineffective in ministry. By sharing these years of his life, Ridge has helped all youth workers remember that the joy and fulfillment of ministering to students is greater than the frustrations and disappointments.

I hope you receive at least a fraction of the benefit from reading this book that I gained from writing it. You may not come to all the same conclusions as Ridge, which is understandable since your personality, gifts, and relationships with others will differ from his. If this book is a success, it will do more than inspire and challenge you, the leader. It will also have an effect on every person with whom you come into contact in your ministry. It is our prayer that such an impact will be made. I hope Ridge and I can work together in another 10 years or so on a new project: *Continue Creating in Me!*

Pam Campbell

CREATE IN ME
A CALLING

SUNDAY, May 23
Ever since last month's staff meeting when the senior pastor, Dave
Owen, asked me if I felt called to youth ministry, I've wondered if this is
what the Lord wants me to do with my life. Before that meeting, I had
never thought much about being called by God to work with high school stu-
dents the rest of my life. I've been asking God to work in my life in such a
way that I will know that call. Well, tonight as I drove home from church, I
think I got an answer to my prayers.
As I drove my little Volkswagen bug down the Southfield freeway, I
really sensed God's presence. I pulled the car over and God seemed to speak
so clearly, saying, "Ridge, I want you to work with students. I'm giving
you the opportunities at Ward Memorial Presbyterian Church so you can do
bigger things for Me in the high school community." I felt really special
and singled out by God. Now I'm wondering what steps the Lord wants me
to take to commit myself to youth ministry.

BEFORE YOU START to think about being a youth pastor, you
must have a personal call by God to youth ministry. It's really key
to be called, make a commitment, and have people affirm that call
in your life.

The point of this chapter is to show how I have tried to live out
my calling to ministry by making the events of my life part of my
preparation for my call. I didn't *have* to travel around to state parks
evangelizing in a milk truck or take a youth ministry job while
going through college. I didn't *have* to work at a private girls' school
while going through seminary, but I knew all these things would
prepare me to be a better youth pastor.

God somehow gives each of us a call either to full-time ministry or to a secular occupation to which we can bring our Christian values and lifestyle. Understanding my call and having others affirm my call have helped me when I feel ambiguous about where I should go and what I should do.

A BRIEF HISTORY

I was born in Detroit, Michigan on September 4, 1951, the youngest of four kids and the only boy.

My dad led me to Christ when I was six years old. When my pastor gave an invitation for people to accept Jesus as their personal Lord and Saviour, I wanted to go forward in the evening service, but my dad wanted me to wait until we could talk. At the next week's service, I made a public profession of faith.

However, in spite of my commitment to Christ, I was a wild kid in church. For instance, once my friends and I disrupted Sunday morning worship by slithering into the baptistry. My faith wasn't really important to me until I got out of high school. A lot of small house churches were started by the Jesus People in my neighborhood, and I participated in several community Bible studies. At the same time I still felt some allegiance to the traditional church because that was where my parents were involved.

I was not a particularly good student in high school. Graduating in the bottom 20 percent of my class, I never even maintained a "C" average in my high school career. In fact, my mom and dad were afraid that I would never graduate. But my values and motivation were not focused on getting good grades. I was more motivated to develop interpersonal skills and relationships.

I played basketball in high school, but the real sport in which I excelled was golf—having played every Saturday with my dad from the age of eight. It took some confidence to be involved in a low-status sport like golf in an inner city school. No one cared about the golf team, so I was the only good golfer at Cooley High.

After graduating from high school I went on an all-summer mission trip with a friend, Dave Horning. This mission trip came out of a spiritual renewal that was taking place in my life. Dave challenged me to go out and do something for God. I decided I wanted to live more like a first-century Christian, so I became more involved in evangelism and a simple lifestyle.

Dave and I bought an old 1957 milk truck and painted "Christ Jesus Is Lord" and "Now Is the Day of Salvation" on its sides. Then we toured the state parks of Michigan, giving children's meetings and evangelistic services each night. We became part of the Jesus People movement, and I found myself becoming very anti-institutional. Because the church represented the institution, and we wanted to base our relationships only on people, not structures, we refused to take money offered for our support by the church missions committee. We even refused to have our ministry dedicated by the church because we saw ourselves as "pioneers for God."

At that point, I felt as if I was on an independent mission from God, believing I didn't really need the church body, that my job was to shake up Christians in my church. Somehow the traditional church didn't seem spiritual enough or on the cutting edge of evangelism. Looking back, I know I came across as flippant, radical, and rebellious toward the church. But I'm glad my church and my family allowed me to be a little radical; they realized that the issues I was dealing with were ultimately going to cause some good things in my life.

While my expressions may have been a little radical, my questions were good ones. For example, I wondered what role the Holy Spirit has in a person's life in the 20th century. I wanted to know if people had to attend church to be Christians. I tried to look beyond the ritual of the church and see real truth.

During our summer trip I learned to live by faith. Each day we didn't know where our next meal was coming from, and yet God faithfully supplied. We took no offerings, but God seemed to provide us with money to keep us going. At one point our truck broke down, and Dave and I were trusting God to keep our summer ministry going. I hitchhiked home to visit my parents in Detroit, and when I arrived, a letter with $90 enclosed was waiting for me. The money took care of our repair bill, and we were thrilled to see God at work in our lives.

When I returned from the mission trip, I entered Wayne State University. A friend asked me to move into a house with five other guys and become a community. We ate meals together, shared directions in which we thought God was leading us, worshiped together each day, and served together. We mowed the neighbor's lawn, shoveled snow off the sidewalks on our street, and painted people's homes. Together, we attempted to serve as a model of what Christian community was all about.

A JOB OFFER

In the course of that year, I was offered the job of youth pastor at Ward Memorial Presbyterian Church in Detroit. Their youth pastor had just left and they were looking for someone involved in evangelism who could capture the interest of the students. Recognizing my skills that were developed during my summer mission trip and because I lived in the community, the church asked me to be their youth pastor. I'd never had a youth pastor or anyone who cared about me from a church standpoint during my high school years, but I was excited that the church would put their students in the trust of a 19-year-old.

I wasn't really sure where to start, but it just seemed natural to develop what I was good at—building relationships. At first, it appeared to be working. The youth group grew to over 100 students almost immediately. The youth program consisted of a small group Sunday School, Wednesday night Bible study, and three retreats a year, and I was responsible to teach every Sunday and Wednesday night. After about 14 months, I began to feel totally overcome with the many responsibilities. Counseling was particularly hard for me. For instance, one girl came to me with sexual problems revolving around her family. Inexperienced in dealing with these kinds of problems, I had very little to say to her. I was ill-prepared, ill-trained, and needed a better base for youth ministry.

One night I shared my frustrations with my housemates—the fact that I wasn't a very good teacher, my time management was terrible, and I was always leaving early or arriving late to classes. I told the guys how difficult I found it to integrate my faith, lifestyle, and work load.

One of the guys suggested that I think about changing schools, recommending Westmont College in Santa Barbara, California. The idea interested me. I'd never thought about spending my life outside the city of Detroit. Suddenly the concept of going to school on the other side of the country became a tremendous challenge. I knew I could be successful in Detroit, but wondered how I would manage on the West Coast which seemed so different and creative. A whole new horizon of opportunities was opening; the sun no longer set on the outskirts of Detroit. My feelings were mixed—a fear of failure combined with great joy about the possibilities.

I began to reevaluate the kind of education I needed, because I felt strongly that God didn't want me to look at youth ministry as a stepping-stone to other forms of ministry. Rather, He desired that I view youth ministry as His plan for my life for the next 10 to 15 years. At Wayne State University, my major was communications. Where my educational goals in the past had been directed toward a career, my new goals were to understand the deeper theological and interpersonal issues that would face a youth pastor involved in the spiritual warfare for high school students. Westmont's philosophy and religion departments looked very appealing. So with my fear of failure and the dream of opportunity, I decided to leave Ward Memorial Presbyterian Church and transfer to Westmont.

WESTMONT COLLEGE

I arrived at Westmont with all my worldly goods in a trunk, suitcase, and garment bag. No one had picked me up at the airport; I didn't know anybody on campus. In fact, the whole school was almost deserted when I got there—the day before the dorms opened. I felt a long way from home. I had gone from being in charge of 100 kids to having no car, no way to get junk food, and no friends. Now I was trapped. Yet in some ways I was still very happy. My loneliness confirmed the fact that I could be a risk-taker and dreamer. It was a dream for an inner-city Detroit boy to go to California to learn about God.

I began spending more time thinking about my call to ministry. My first thoughts were to get involved in ministry while I was still in college. I tried a few things like dorm Bible studies and teaching Sunday School, but I was too busy. I needed time to think through

I'M READY FOR A YOUTH MINISTRY!

and prepare for ministry.

While studying religion and philosophy at Westmont, I learned that God was not as simplistic as I had made Him out to be. And because I was in an environment where people respected the institutional church, I learned that the local church *was* a legitimate place to minister. I found the West Coast churches to be more renewal-oriented than churches I'd previously experienced, and they seemed to minister more personally to me. Westmont helped me discover answers to my questions about the legitimacy of the institutional church and how relationships with God fit into church history. Again, God was preparing me for ministry through the questions and resources of Westmont.

ROOMMATES

God gave me two roommates, Bruce Bugbee and Corbin Hillam. Corb, Bruce, and I lived together for two-and-a-half years at Westmont. An artist, Corb viewed things creatively; where I might see logistics, he saw colors, shapes, and hues. Bruce, on the other hand, was a fighter. His father died while we were in college, so he was always grappling with trying to pay for school and do well in classes. His perspective was one of survival while mine was that of a dreamer.

These two roommates helped me begin to see things not as they are, but as they could be. Corb would critique a chapel speaker on eloquence and the word pictures the speaker painted. Bruce would evaluate the same chapel speaker on content, while I critiqued the speaker's ability to motivate me to do better things for God. God put the three of us together to rub off on each other. In a true sense, I am what I am today because of the roommates God gave me.

For our entire time at Westmont, Corb, Bruce, and I lived in Lauren House, a freshman dorm that had the least status on campus. Even as seniors we felt we had a responsibility to make that dorm better than its reputation. One way we accomplished that was through the Spring Sing—a sort of musical theater competition put on by students for the community. The whole campus would participate with seven or eight dorm groups performing 10-minute musicals complete with band, backdrops, costumes, and lighting. Lauren House had always finished last in Spring Sing, but during our senior year, Corb, Bruce, and I decided to win.

Working with the theme of "Occupations," we chose to be professional tooth fairies. In our skit the Mafia tried to prevent the tooth fairies from giving a quarter to a little boy who had just lost his tooth. We changed the words to "The Unsinkable Molly Brown" and the theme of "Hogan's Heroes" and found that when we sang those two together, they matched perfectly.

We practiced for hours. Corb dreamed what it would look like while Bruce worked out the theme. We needed help with the music, so even though I'd never directed a choir, I volunteered to be music director. We found some guys to arrange music and play in a band. At each practice, we prayed together, asking God to use this Spring Sing to bring our dorm together spiritually. We ended up winning the Spring Sing, and as we gave our acceptance speeches, we were able to testify about what God had done in our dorm.

Though this was just a fun college experience, it gave me confidence and helped prepare me to lead kids in areas in which I had no expertise. I was not a song leader, yet I was able to pull it off. I discovered that I could be part of a theater group even though I was not an actor. In the same way, I knew I could be a youth pastor even though I knew little about pastoring youth.

ROBANNE

I had only one semester to establish a solid relationship with my roommates before meeting Robanne. She came to Westmont having spent one semester abroad in Europe. The first time I saw Robanne was at the post office. She was surrounded by a pack of girls, but she apparently also had a lot of friends who were guys. I asked my buddies who she was and, from that moment on, they thought I ought to date her. Later, I was studying in the library and Robanne came by. I was wearing a Michigan sweatshirt, so I covered up all the letters of Michigan with my hands except the "h" and the "i." She was impressed enough to go out with me.

As we got to know each other, we prayed together and shared common dreams. I soon realized that Robanne was a girl who was serious about her faith. It didn't take long for Robanne and me to fall in love. She was a sociology major studying to be an elementary education teacher, but she had worked for her youth pastor as his secretary and was really involved in youth ministry. I began spending every weekend at her house which was just two hours from Santa Barbara, and her parents became my second family.

Robanne's and my relationship was built primarily on letters and the hours we spent together talking. Our decision to get married came after a lot of thinking through what God wanted us to do cooperatively. For example, we spent some time apart before we

HOW TO CHOOSE A SEMINARY

1. *Write out your goals in terms of your occupation.* All schools have certain strengths and weaknesses. Seminary faculties change and flex over the years. Some schools that were very strong in Christian education 10 years ago are very weak right now. Compare your goals with the stated purposes of the seminary.

2. *Look at the product that the seminary has produced.* Examine the graduates of the school and the kinds of churches most graduates are called to. If you want to go into a Southern Baptist church, it's going to be very difficult for you to achieve that unless you go to a Southern Baptist seminary. Look at the kinds of churches and ministries that recent graduates involve themselves in. Ask yourself if those are the kinds of ministries you would want to be involved with.

3. *Believe in the limits of seminary education.* The classroom experience that a seminary offers is only part of your education. Look at the surrounding community and the ministry opportunities available to you while you're in seminary.

got married. That time simply confirmed that it was God's will for us to get together. The decision to go to seminary was agreed on prior to our marriage.

After graduating from Westmont, I needed a job in order to get married. For nine months I worked as a shipping clerk in a Los Angeles sports equipment factory where most of the employees were Mexicans. Since I was the only person in the factory who spoke English, I was promoted to head of the shipping department because all the truck drivers spoke English. Even at this point in my life, God began to prepare me for ministries with Mexican-Americans.

SEMINARY
When we enrolled in Trinity Evangelical Divinity School, Robanne and I made the long trek across the country to Deerfield, Illinois. We felt the rush of adventure—ready to be on our own, pursuing

dreams without the proximity of our families. However, the adventure was nothing like what I expected it to be.

I expected seminary to be an institution where warm, comfortable, stimulating groups of committed Christians loved each other—almost a spiritual womb. To my surprise, seminary was full of three kinds of people. One group seemed to be made up of people who were not called to ministry but who were exploring ministry. Many in this first group had been unsuccessful in the secular world, yet they believed God could use them, so they were exploring ministry and getting their training. The second group appeared to consist of people whose parents had envisioned their children as preachers, and therefore had directed them toward ministry. The third group included people who were serious about their faith and really wanted to be ministers. I never saw that group on campus; they came to classes and then they were gone. I soon came to believe that seminary was a place where you went to class, and then if you were ministry-directed, you went out to minister the rest of the time, trying to balance studies with ministry. There was a real dichotomy between those who were going to seminary for academic reasons and those who were getting training for ministry.

Robanne and I only wanted to fit into the third category, so we began to look for a ministry. Robanne was my partner in learning—splitting her time between a job and auditing several classes with me so we could grow together. Eventually we got a job as house parents at Ferry Hall, a boarding school for girls in Lake Forest, Illinois.

Most of the girls at Ferry Hall came from wealthy homes, and our responsibilities included discipline, encouragement, affirmation, and tutoring. We were in charge of 35 ninth- and tenth-grade girls, 24 hours a day, seven days a week. We got one weekend off a month, and one evening off a week. It was a tough job for a couple who had only been married one year. Not only did this one-year-old marriage suddenly have 35 offspring, but those offspring were all 14- and 15-year-old females.

Most of those girls didn't know God from Donald Duck. They were hard-core non-Christian girls, looking for love, affection, and their own identities. It was not unusual to see limousines pick the girls up on a Friday night and return them on Sunday night because their parents didn't care enough to come and pick them up.

Sex, drugs, abortion, and suicide became real problems to me.

They were no longer issues that we just talked about in seminary. The girls elected me to the court, a group of faculty members and students who settled all disciplinary problems. This was a little unusual since I was more conservative than most of the other dorm parents. My election seemed to affirm that Robanne and I were good at our jobs. The time we spent at Ferry Hall as dorm parents was probably the best training we've had for youth ministry.

One of the things that Ferry Hall made me good at was justice and discipline. I had to come up with a plan for how to discipline kids on a regular basis. For example, I told the girls that they could tell me anything and I would believe them and do everything I could to help them, but they had better not lie to me.

The more I got involved in Ferry Hall, the less I got involved in Trinity. My advisor called me into his office one day and encouraged me to change my lifestyle, rhetoric, and attitude. I think what he was really trying to say was, "Ridge, you don't fit into the Trinity community." I wore shorts to class while other students wore suits and ties. I didn't carry a briefcase; I carried a backpack. I didn't enjoy discussing theology at the local coffee shop. My advisor's perception of me seemed to be, "Ridge, you'd be better off if you took full advantage of the seminary environment."

While my lifestyle bothered my advisor, it was a trophy to me. I didn't want to fit into the seminary community, even though Trinity was a very, very good school. I was in the academic setting because I knew it was going to make me a better youth pastor. However, most youth pastors are trying to create programs that smack against the youth culture, so it's not all bad to be in a subtle state of rebellion. I was not comfortable in an academic setting because I was always itching to get out and actually minister to others. Again, I don't fit well into institutions because I'm a dreamer, and ritualism and politics grate on my creativity. That attitude has plagued me in all of my ministry.

INTERNSHIP ·

Most of my friends did their internships at Evangelical Free churches because Trinity is an EFC seminary. They went to small churches where they had lots of power, perhaps even total responsibility for the church and its youth program for the summer. They felt this would give them a real handle on ministry.

I disagreed with this idea that an internship should be a comfortable position in which the intern takes his skills to the church and helps the congregation. Rather, I think it should be viewed as a position in which a person is challenged and stretched to be progressive and think beyond his current skills and strengths.

Robanne and I began to pray about where we would do our internship. We decided to go to a large church where little participation would be expected of us, but where we could observe the important aspects of ministry. Choosing the right church was critical. Which one would meet our needs? I thought of Dr. Malcolm Cronk who had been a professor at Trinity and one of the pastors of the church that we attended. Now he was the pastor of the Church of the Open Door in Los Angeles, California. I wrote and asked if I could be his intern for the summer.

Dr. Cronk's reply was yes. He wanted me to be an intern, but the church couldn't pay my expenses. Suddenly, we were faced not only with the expenses of a 2,000-mile trip, but also the cost of the seminary class. Though most of our friends at Trinity were taking paid internships, Robanne and I felt that the training and knowledge we would receive at the Church of the Open Door was worth the expense. We worked out some of our financial concerns by living with Robanne's parents during the summer, giving Robanne some time with her family while I learned about ministry.

In one summer, Dr. Cronk revealed what it was like to be a pastor. He showed me letters that criticized him, as well as board minutes, and memos by staff members. He allowed me to be a part of some difficult situations because he knew that I'd have to swim over the same water sometime. For example, one time an elder called Dr. Cronk to complain about one of the staff members. I offered to leave Dr. Cronk's office, but he put the man on hold and said, "Here's a situation where you can listen to my side of the story to see how I defend and support staff members." He was right; I learned from that experience.

He showed me an excellent model of expositional preaching and how to motivate a church to be missions-minded. He allowed me to participate in elders' meetings and guided me through the mechanism of the church. One instance really opened my eyes to the realities of pastoring. Dr. Cronk had preached one of the best sermons I'd ever heard. Two days later, he showed me a letter from a church member accusing him of not being biblical or relevant. I knew that Dr. Cronk had touched my life that Sunday, and I thought, *How can it be? How can I be so touched by this message and another member write this nasty note?* I discovered that was what ministry was like, and Dr. Cronk was open enough to share it with me.

Someone else who shared his life with me was Mark Newenshwander, the college pastor at Church of the Open Door. He was such a creative guy it almost scared me. Even his home was a total brushstroke of creativity—the colors, furniture, and landscaping. His clothes, office, method of speaking, and style of ministry were slightly different from everybody else's. When he participated on the platform, his calls to worship and pastoral prayers were either very contemporary or incredibly old and classic. Finally I had to sit down with Mark and ask, "Why do you do things differently? Why don't you conform?"

"Ridge," Mark replied, "when I participate in worship, I want to use a form that people are going to take notice of. I want them to remember *what* I had to say because of *how* I said it." He explained that a lot of people say very good things, but they don't say them in a way that makes people want to listen.

After talking with Mark, I was challenged to develop my own style of teaching—not using a seminary model—and become comfortable with my own style of innovation and creativity. I came away from that internship with a real understanding that my style is not to fit into my surroundings, but to make my surroundings fit into my life.

CONFIRMATION OF A CALLING

After three years, my Trinity education came to an end and it was time to select a church. I was surprised at the constant stream of pastors who visited Trinity. The Advice-givers came with their agendas—trying to tell seminarians what they needed to do to be successful in any church. Then the Salesmen would say, "If you'd like to participate in our church, we've got a great experience." The kinds of pastors that I appreciated were the ones who were simply interested in me as a person. They realized that programs come out of the heart.

I was also surprised at how slowly churches moved in making personnel decisions. Very few churches say, "You're our man" in two weeks. And that's very frustrating for a seminarian who is itching to be involved in ministry.

Though contacted by lots of churches, I focused in on three—in Dallas, San Diego, and San Francisco. The first interview was with Chuck Wickman, senior pastor of the Evangelical Free Church of Walnut Creek (near San Francisco). About two minutes into my interview, I knew I was going to Walnut Creek. I liked Chuck immediately and felt a peace about what he told me. Walnut Creek also fit my criteria for selecting a church.

First, I knew I had to recognize my limitations. While I really wanted to go to a church of 2,000-3,000 members with a youth group of 200-300 (being of the "bigger is better" mindset), I knew that I couldn't handle a group that large. So I set my goal for a group of about 50 students. I liked Walnut Creek because it was a middle-sized church and met that goal.

A second criterion was that I get along with the senior pastor. Chuck and I hit it off well, and I knew we could build a friendship. He was creative; I *liked* him. I know a lot of people say, "Don't go on your feelings because they can change," but I've usually been able to trust my feelings, discerning in my heart whether a situation will work. And this felt right.

My third criterion was to ask a lot of questions. I called a lot of people about the Walnut Creek church, talking to some members of the congregation and interviewing as many people as possible to be satisfied that Walnut Creek was where God wanted me to be.

I think Chuck Wickman did some talking too. When I arrived to candidate at the church, the first thing he and I did was play golf. From that point I didn't care what the kids or church looked like—I was ready to come to the church because I knew we had something

---

CALLED TO THE MINISTRY

How do you know when you're called to the ministry?

1. *The calling is confirmed by the Holy Spirit.* A pastor should have a real sense that God is dealing with him. When you're called by God, your perspective, goals, and visions change to fit that call.

2. *The calling is confirmed by godly men and women.* Men like Dave Horning and Dr. Cronk confirmed the fact that I was called by God. Ask people you respect to confirm your calling.

3. *The calling is confirmed by a congregation of God's people.* You should see some results of your calling. God will fulfill your calling through actual ministry. The result does not have to be measured in numbers, but it does have to evidence a real-life situation where you begin to see God working and using you to change lives.

fun we could do together.

Robanne and I hadn't been candidating at Walnut Creek very long when we looked at each other and said, "This is where we should be." After praying about it for a couple of weeks, on the day of the graduation ceremony at Trinity, I called up Chuck Wickman and told him that I'd like to be his youth pastor.

PASTORS IN TRAINING

The Pastors in Training (P.I.T.) program is an internship program that enables the church staff to share what they have learned and what God has entrusted to them with the young men and women who are called by God into the ministry. The program exposes them to the lives and ministries of pastors in local churches, giving them a taste of the hurts and joys, the strengths and weaknesses.

Qualifications

In order to participate in the P.I.T. Program, a person must have the following qualifications:

1. He must be willing to make a commitment for 12 months.

2. He must have as his goal full-time Christian service.

3. He must be committed to the pastoral ministry in the local church.

4. He must have completed two years of college or Bible school.

5. He must commit himself to a minimum of 20 hours per week.

Responsibilities

The P.I.T. Program is divided into three parts: general requirements, a major requirement, and personal requirements.

The General Requirements
The basic requirements will take approximately 8 hours of the 20-hour work week.

1. Staff Meetings—The P.I.T. must commit himself to meeting with the pastoral staff at their regular staff meetings.

2. Pulpit Exposure—Depending on the skills and goals of the P.I.T., pulpit exposure will be encouraged, perhaps involving the reading of Scripture or prayer in the worship service.

3. Worship Planning and Participation—The P.I.T. will be asked to help in the planning of Worship Services.

4. Goal-setting—The P.I.T. will set weekly, monthly, quarterly, and yearly goals, to be reviewed by the supervising pastor.

5. Time Management—The P.I.T. will be required to fill out a weekly schedule sheet.

6. Visitation—The P.I.T. will be exposed to all areas of pastoral care. During the year, the P.I.T. should make a minimum of 15 calls in each of the following areas: member calls; inactive member calls; shut-in calls; hospital calls; and calls on the general congregation of the church. The P.I.T. will also assist in times of bereavement, premarital counseling, counseling of the terminally ill, communion in the home, mental illness, and family and personal crisis counseling.

7. Budget Preparation—The P.I.T. will be involved in budget-setting.

8. Polity—The P.I.T. should attend all monthly board meetings. Attendance is also required at the annual meeting of the church and any congregational meetings.

9. Information Gathering—The P.I.T. will gather information toward a paper he will be writing, titled, "How I See This Church."

10. Staff Awareness—The P.I.T. is required to read, research, evaluate, and discuss the present job descriptions of each staff member.

The Major Requirement
In order to better understand his individual strengths and weaknesses, the P.I.T. needs to focus on a major. The basic ingredients for a major will consume a minimum of 10 hours per week.

1. The Project—The P.I.T. is required to choose a project of lasting value. It may be research-oriented, a physical project, or a program of training leadership.

2. Staff Meetings—The P.I.T. will meet with his supervising staff members once a week. This meeting will involve discussion of some of the books being read by the P.I.T. in his personal study. At this staff meeting, he will discuss goals for his major and tailor-make a program for that major.

3. Administrative Responsibilities—The P.I.T. is required to take on some administrative responsibility that will give him an overview of the church. It must involve more

than one age-group of people.

4. Counseling—The P.I.T. should facilitate counseling times with the people with whom he is working, and be able to have those counseling experiences evaluated by his supervising pastor.

5. Teaching—The P.I.T. is required to be involved in some aspect of weekly teaching.

The Personal Requirements
The personal requirements of the P.I.T. Program require approximately two hours a week and involve three aspects.

1. Required Reading—Some good books for required reading are *Life Together* by Dietrich Bonhoeffer; *Knowing God* by J.I. Packer; *Sharpening the Focus of the Church* by Gene Getz; *Effective Teaching* by Larry Richards; *The Measure of the Church* by Gene Getz; *The Golden Calf* by John White; *The Strong-Willed Child* by James Dobson; *The Knowledge of the Holy* by A.W.Tozer; and *Rich Christians in an Age of Hunger* by Ronald Sider.

2. The Log—The P.I.T. is required to keep a daily log of his time schedule as well as his impressions, feelings, frustrations, and thoughts about his participation in the program. This log will be reviewed with the supervising pastor on a bi-weekly basis.

3. The Paper—As a climax to the P.I.T. Program, the P.I.T. is required to put down in concise fashion his thoughts about how he sees the church. The research paper should be 12-15 pages, due the final day of the internship. It will be reviewed by the entire pastoral staff.

The Church's Responsibilities to the P.I.T.

The pastoral staff must commit themselves to being open, honest, and approachable. Their goal should be to allow free access to the workings of the church so the P.I.T. will be prepared to step into a pastoral ministry upon completion of his education and the P.I.T. program. It is their responsibility to pray for the P.I.T. as well as provide him with honest evaluations and recommendations for future ministries. The church bears responsibility and accountability for the P.I.T's spiritual nurture during his participation in this program. Following is a sample contract to be signed and returned by the P.I.T.

The Pastor in Training Contract

Name _____

Address _____

Phone _____

The P.I.T. Program begins on _____ (Date) _____

and terminates on _____ (Date) _____ The

supervising pastor for your program is _____

The church will provide $_____ per month
toward your living expenses. Any church event in which
you participate will be paid for by the church.

_____
Supervising Pastor

_____
Date

_____
Participant in P.I.T. Program

SMALL CHURCH SPOTLIGHT

PAM: Ridge, how important should seminary be to the volunteer or lay youth worker who is considering a career change to full-time youth ministry?

RIDGE: First of all, don't go to seminary unless you're called to the ministry. Seminary is not geared to explore whether or not you're called. It's there because you *are* called.

PAM: I agree! Whether a full-time youth pastor or a part-time volunteer, you still have to be called to youth work. The first question I ask my volunteers is, "Are you called to work with students?" If they say yes, then we can start working together.

RIDGE: This may sound incongruous, but I think it's very important to have a seminary degree if you plan to go into full-time youth ministry. Seminary may not teach you ministry, but it gives you some instant credibility. I could not have my current job position if I didn't have a seminary degree. As I mentioned in this chapter, I'm not a youth pastor *because* of seminary; I was a youth pastor *before* I went to seminary. Seminary just helped to refine me into a better youth pastor.

PAM: Too many people seem to go to seminary to become youth pastors. If you're not ministering to people before you go, you're not going to after you get a degree.

RIDGE: Part-timers shouldn't look down on themselves because they don't have seminary or don't have, according to some people, the appropriate or best preparation for youth ministry. Some of my best volunteers are school teachers. If they're involved in any form of education, they can interpret educational principles and use them in ministry.

PAM: If a person is going to seminary, how important is it for him to be involved in ministry while he's going to school?

RIDGE: Extremely important, because then he can begin to write papers and ask questions that are practical! It's easy to get on a tangent about whether the first few chapters of Genesis are to be taken literally or figuratively, and then believe that this tangent is an important issue for the church. However, students don't care about that issue. But they might care about the whole evolutionary process, and then you can use what you learned in seminary.

Once I knew I was called to youth ministry, if I had a choice about a topic for a paper in school, I would choose something that dealt with students to help me in my ministry. I made sure all my class work integrated with my daily experiences with students.

PAM: What kind of education or experience does a lay person need to work with students?

RIDGE: While my education and experience was all directed toward my occupation, volunteers need to take the education and environment they bring to the youth program and capitalize on that to form the body of Christ.

two
CREATE IN ME
SELF-CONFIDENCE

MONDAY, July 8

Today, a huge Mayflower van pulled up outside our little two-bedroom apartment at Trinity seminary in Deerfield, Illinois. As the morning passed, I watched all our earthly belongings fill up about three feet of floor space in the back end of the van. Then Robanne and I loaded up our car and began the long drive to California.

As we wheel across the country, Robanne and I plan to talk about our dreams and goals for the future. Robanne has never seen me in a ministry before. We've worked together at seminary, but this will be the first time that we team together for a ministry. I wonder how we will relate to each other outside an academic setting.

Next week, I'll begin my new job as associate pastor/student ministries at the Evangelical Free Church of Walnut Creek. I feel really confident that we made a good decision. Every day I'm realizing that Robanne and I are just beginning to learn how to work together.

I wonder how Robanne and I will fit in at Walnut Creek. Will we be equipped to meet the church's youth ministry needs? We have seminary training, but is that enough? Where do we start? What do we do? How do we begin a youth ministry?

WHEN A BASKETBALL TEAM goes into the gym with the expectation that they will win, they usually win. If they go out on the court tentatively, they usually don't win. They end up spending half the game just trying to get their game plan together. The same thing is true of a youth pastor. In order to succeed, he must go into youth work with some kind of confidence that he can do the job. But that doesn't happen naturally. He has to work at acquiring self-confidence and measure that confidence through a few victories.

A lack of self-confidence manifests itself in discipline problems. One of the things that I've seen across the country as I've traveled and spoken is that groups with discipline problems usually have a youth pastor who does not have the ability (or self-confidence) to program effectively. He runs around tentatively trying to control the situation instead of taking charge. So self-confidence gives a youth pastor the ability to take charge of his ministry.

Overconfidence isn't usually a problem in the first years of youth ministry. However, as a youth pastor becomes more self-confident, he can steamroll kids with ideas to a point that it eventually catches up with him and makes him insensitive. I'm guilty of that. For example, I've been on so many retreats that I have a tendency to be overconfident that I can make a retreat work without bringing God into the process. There have been retreats where a kid really needed to talk to me, and rather than talking with this kid, I hid myself in tasks. I'm sometimes overconfident about the whole program so that I don't think I need to minister to the individual needs of kids.

In this chapter, I want to illustrate how the people who hire a youth pastor hire him with the expectation that he is a confident expert. I entered my ministry at the Evangelical Free Church of Walnut Creek, California with seminary experience, but I really didn't have a lot of confidence. The perceptions of the people who hired me and my self-perception were in conflict.

A LACK OF CONFIDENCE
As I think back to this year of ministry, I know now that Robanne and I had no clues as to what the future held for us. We had no understanding of the time demands and the constraints youth ministry would place on our marriage.

When we arrived in Walnut Creek, we quietly moved into the apartment that the church had helped us select. Then we headed down to the Evangelical Free Church to have coffee with the pastor and meet the rest of the staff. I felt nervous because I knew I didn't know the ropes—sort of like a kid on his first day of high school. I fit in because the church had called me and made an investment in my move, but I didn't know what kind of authority I would have or what kind of structures were in the church.

When I met my secretary, I thought to myself, *I had to pay someone to type my papers at seminary! Now the church is going to pay someone to make my life easier.* I really didn't know how to use a secretary but was thrilled to discover that she would do my typing, answer my phone, and secure buses for trips.

After describing some of the office procedures, my secretary showed me into my office. I'd worked in factories, schools, and academic situations, but none of my previous jobs had ever been in an office. I didn't even know what a dictaphone was! And I certainly didn't know how to work a copy machine, particularly one that reduced. Office work was all new to me.

THE VALUE OF A SECRETARY

Most seminaries don't have a course on how to work with a secretary. If you're worried about how to use a secretary or if you feel unprepared to keep your secretary busy, here are some ideas on what your secretary /assistant can do for you as a youth pastor. Encourage your secretary to:

1. Pray for you.
2. Encourage you.
3. Listen.
4. Offer suggestions based on experience.
5. Give feedback and be a sounding board regarding your youth program.
6. Organize your work load, take phone calls, and take care of as many details as possible.
7. Make you look good . . . or better, if necessary.

In return, show your secretary that you value her experience and skills by:

1. Giving her all pertinent, correct details and information. Then, when you're out of the office, she'll be able to give out correct information to students, parents, staff, and anyone else trying to reach you.
2. Asking your secretary to come into your office to discuss the jobs you have for her to do. Allowing interruptions or mumbling information to your secretary as you run out the door is rude and can create some major conflicts in your relationship and your ministry.
3. Working with your secretary in a team approach, discussing events and issues. A secretary/assistant needs to feel needed beyond the capacity of typing and taking messages. A team approach will add a whole new dimension to her job.

Looking at the bare office walls, I was glad that I had been to seminary. I had picked up enough books in school to fill the empty bookshelves. *At least that would make me look smart,* I thought. Unpacking my books, putting them on the shelves, buying desk organizers, and hanging pictures on the walls were just nervous reactions. I felt as if I was in school, starting a new semester. Of course, my newly-framed seminary diploma went on a wall where people could see it when they walked in. I wanted my office to look impressive. After all, the only model that I had was the senior pastor's office, and it looked like the Library of Congress. When everything was in place, I shut the door and sat down. In the quiet I thought—and worried.

What do I do now? How do I start a youth ministry? I had created the facade of being a "together" youth pastor, but I knew that my job was more than an organized office. As I sat at my desk, I realized that what I saw in that office was not ministry. Ministry had to take place in my heart and in my ability to relate to kids. I began to feel the awesome responsibility of a youth ministry. Stunned, I thought, *These church people are paying me to do something about which I really have no confidence or knowledge!*

UNDERSTANDING MY ROLE
Having begun my ministry without any set plan, I figured the best way to understand my role as youth pastor was to see how *students* defined my role. I knew that I could be a success if I met and fulfilled their expectations. Kids are the bottom line. If the kids are happy, they communicate positive things to their parents, and the parents communicate positive things to the church.

My secretary gave me a current mailing list of the students, and I made dozens of phone calls. Asking questions and using word associations helped me get a handle on their feelings about Sunday School, the church, the senior pastor, their families, and my role as youth pastor. Through this survey I gained a ton of helpful information. It was also a comfortable way for me to introduce myself and get to know the church's young people.

When I called the kids, their first reaction was total disbelief and shock. They said, "Why are you calling me?" Some were genuinely moved that I would take the time to call them. I'd say, "I hate to talk over the phone. Could we get together tomorrow? I'll come over to your house and pick you up." The reaction was defensiveness. Then when the kids found out they weren't in trouble, they got really excited.

As my profile of Walnut Creek students developed, I found out these kids didn't particularly like Sunday School or social events. What they really wanted were personal relationships. Most of them came from good families, not broken homes. I discovered that while school was very important, athletics were not.

Secondly, I found that different students had different expectations for their youth pastor. Some thought I should be personally involved with every aspect of their lives. Others were threatened by me. A leaderless program had given them an excuse for not getting involved in church. These threatened kids had enjoyed the fact that the youth program was not doing very well before I came. They answered my survey questions in a sarcastic tone that said, "Don't get too close to me." If I asked them a question about their spiritual walk—"What do you think of falling in love with Christ?"—they would say, "I'm not really into this church thing."

Finally, the more I talked with students, the more I understood that being a youth pastor means being a self-starter. In seminary, I had gotten the impression that kids would flock to me with creative ideas for social events, retreats, and programs. It didn't happen that way. Instead, I would ask a Walnut Creek kid, "What kind of socials would you like?" and he would reply, "I don't know." I asked a girl if she were a youth pastor what she would do. "I don't know," she replied. "Just do what you're doing, I guess. Try to get to know us."

When I realized that students were relying on me to create their programs and ministries, I got excited—and nervous. I could shape these kids and their programs into whatever I wanted them to be. The church had left me to chart my own course. On the other hand, I didn't know if I was prepared to do that.

Coming from an academic setting, I was used to examining each semester's syllabus, reading the right books, writing papers, taking tests, and receiving a well-deserved grade in the course. At Walnut Creek, the senior pastor had no syllabus for me, the board of elders expected me to set my own schedule, and the Christian Education Committee looked to me for direction and guidance. The only clear directive I had from the church was that I—the youth pastor—was primarily responsible for making sure their kids were spiritually fed.

Before long I found myself facing demands on my time, energy, creativity, and personal life. Suddenly I was responsible for Sunday School and Wednesday night Bible study. At the same time, I felt obliged to be at every football game, every basketball game, and

SURVEYING YOUR STUDENTS

Want to find out how your youth view you? Use the following survey to get a reading on your students' perceptions of the church, Sunday School, the senior pastor, their family situations, and your role.

1. How do you respond to the following statements? Circle the number that applies for each. (1—strongly disagree, 2—disagree, 3—undecided /don't know, 4—agree, 5—strongly agree)

- Our church effectively meets the needs of youth.   1 2 3 4 5
- Our youth group takes good care of its members.   1 2 3 4 5
- I feel that the youth pastor will listen if I go to him with a problem.   1 2 3 4 5
- I have sufficient opportunities to use my talents and gifts for the good of the church or youth group.   1 2 3 4 5
- Communication between the youth pastor and students needs to be improved.   1 2 3 4 5
- Bible studies or Sunday School classes are relevant and applicable to my daily life.   1 2 3 4 5
- Peace, unity, and oneness exist between youth group members.   1 2 3 4 5

2. What comes to mind when you think about:
Sunday School
Your family
Your school
The senior pastor
The youth pastor

Demographics
3. Member of church?
4. Age
5. Male __ Female __
6. Attend church
7. Attend Sunday School
8. Attend youth group/Bible study
9. Additional comments

every track meet. The responsibility for the spiritual life of 65 high school students weighed heavily on Robanne and me. If Robanne and I prayed together or were disciplined in our Bible study, kids would mimic our actions in a positive way. However, there was always the danger that kids might pick up on other not-so-desirable habits in our lives. Kids became interested in what radio stations we listened to, what movies we went to, whether we drank wine, whether we were involved in sexual relationships before we got married.

Suddenly our personal lives were on display. Once Robanne was sitting in the back of a van where I couldn't really hear her entire conversation with the students. One of the kids crawled up to the front where I was driving and said, "Boy, you should hear what Robanne is telling us about you!" I knew Robanne was saying good things about me, but I could also tell from the kids' faces in the rearview mirror that they were really listening. They were learning from our model. The kids' expectations were reasonable, but Robanne and I were unprepared for the responsibilities that went with them.

The demands on my time were unbelievable. In seminary, a youth pastor is taught to guard his day off and make sure he spends time with his family. That is very important, but I think many of my contemporaries go overboard trying to protect themselves in this area. They don't realize that the job of youth pastor is designed to have huge time demands placed on it. It's a big job.

Prior to this ministry, I had never taught a Bible study on a regular basis. In less than a month, I ran out of key illustrations, and my favorite talks were gone. In seminary, I had listened to wise professors' lectures and tried to duplicate their lessons in my own life. Suddenly, I didn't have that kind of input in my life. I had to learn to study the Bible on my own and to come up with outlines from Scripture, relying on what the Holy Spirit was teaching me.

As the demands of youth ministry piled up, I saw that my seminary education was inadequate. I was not fully equipped for the task before me. Somehow the Greek and Hebrew I had struggled to learn seemed far away and useless. The Walnut Creek kids needed to understand issues like abortion, premarital sex, and alcohol and drug abuse from practical as well as biblical viewpoints. Coming from an academic setting, I had trouble working in a practical setting. I wanted to give the kids theological answers for their social problems and concerns, but students wanted practical answers to questions like, "What do I say to a girl who has had an abortion?" Suddenly, my "Sanctity of Life" course at Trinity didn't make a lot of sense.

CULTURAL GUIDES

In our first year at Walnut Creek, Robanne and I not only had to adjust to our new ministry roles; we also worked to adjust to California culture. California was very different from the Midwest—in everything from architecture to fashion to lifestyles. In the Midwest, we had driven an eight-year-old Dodge Dart, and we were envied by everyone in the seminary. When we drove it around California, it was no big deal. In the Midwest, people were very hospitable and had often invited us into their homes. In California, we felt isolated, unable to build relationships.

Up to this point, in seminary and in the way we had lived our lives, there were not many expectations placed on Robanne. Now while I was struggling to meet students' expectations, Robanne was suddenly faced with expectations associated with the role of any youth pastor's wife. Everyone wanted Robanne's time. People asked her to play the piano, sing solos, lead Bible studies, and speak at Women's Missionary Fellowship meetings. Within the first couple of weeks of ministry, Robanne had to decide whether these were good choices or reasonable expectations. Should she lead a Bible study, be involved in women's ministries, and participate in women's prayer groups, or strictly work with the student ministries? She decided to simply work with high school students.

Both of us felt swamped. We needed help—friends who could help us adjust to our new lives and understand California and the Walnut Creek church. Enter Bev and Jim Linman, who had three sons in high school—and a *van*. Jim, a man with the gift of giving, often allowed us to borrow his van for church trips. Robanne and I soon became close friends with Jim and Bev. In their own way, Jim and Bev were Midwest-type people. They were stable, caring, and loving. Plus they had the gift of hospitality. We began to share meals on a regular basis, and soon were getting together almost daily.

Jim and Bev became our cultural guides. Even though they were a few years older than we were, age didn't separate us and we enjoyed a totally open relationship with them. They had been at Walnut Creek church for a long time, and we were able to share our frustrations and ask questions that we could not ask anyone else at the church. We could trust Bev and Jim to be honest and keep our discussions confidential. Because of their willingness to open their home and their lives to us, we understood more fully why the church, and Californians, functioned the way they did. The Linmans were part of the "old school" of the church; Jim was on the pulpit committee and was very well respected by church members. In some ways, linking with Jim allowed me to have more of an acceptance with the whole congregation.

Just as Bev and Jim introduced us to the church and California life, two students served as cultural guides to the local high schools. I asked the Lord to give me a student or two who would be willing to help me understand the students at the church. The Lord answered that prayer when Dave Courtney and Sue Austin came into my office one day just to say they were glad I was there, and that they wanted to be my friends. They seemed to want to tell me a few things, so I asked them to explain California kids to me. Almost immediately, they became my cultural guides. Dave and I visited 20 or 30 students to find out what their homes were like. Sue took me to football games and the local hangouts.

Even though she was a student, Sue became my shepherd—not spiritually, but in the area of sociological development. At this point in my ministry, I had the attitude that students were the learners and I was the teacher. But I found that Sue had a lot more to say to me than I had to say to her because she could help me understand the environment in which God had placed me to minister.

Dave and Sue helped keep me from looking totally inept during one of the first events that I programmed at Walnut Creek—a college tour. I'd spent a great deal of time explaining to the kids the importance of keeping on schedule. Of course, on the day the tour was scheduled to leave, I overslept. The treasurer of the church finally called to see what happened to me. I hurried to church where I found 30 parents waiting in the parking lot for my arrival. Imagine my embarrassment at trying to establish my image as an organized youth pastor, only to blow it on my first trip. It could have been a horrible situation, but Dave and Sue were there to run interference for me. They were my great defenders, and their opinions went a long way with the parents.

LIMITED PERSPECTIVES

One of the limited perspectives I encountered during this year of youth ministry was coping with the "messiah mentality"—a peculiar phenomenon in which parents expect that the youth pastor will correct all the problems of their children. Some of my students' parents expected me to provide instant programs and establish great rapport with each of their kids. To some parents, I became a "messiah" who could wipe away all their son's or daughter's problems. It seemed I was expected to make a young "Billy Graham" out of each student who might be involved with drug and alcohol abuse.

The majority of parents, like Jim and Bev Linman, did not expect me to be perfect. They wanted me to be who I was. Unfortunately, their support wasn't voiced as loudly as the criticism of parents who were saying, "This guy can't seem to relate to my son."

I was also bothered by the limited perspectives toward Walnut Creek's youth program. While my programs were aimed at the broad range of student needs, some parents' expectations focused strictly on how I related to *their* children. Some parents evaluated my success or failure solely on whether or not *their* kids were interested or involved in church activities . . . and some of these kids could not have cared less about church. Yet these parents didn't see that a program could be good even though their sons or daughters did not relate well to it.

Dr. Lloyd Perry, my professor of pastoral theology at Trinity, had given me some advice on beginning a youth ministry: "Do something that will guarantee you a victory so you can stake your claim on the church." With parents who measured victory in terms of their own children, I wondered how I could stake my claim on Walnut Creek.

Another limited perspective in my ministry was my own. I hadn't realized that being a youth pastor meant that I would become an instant role model for students. I was overwhelmed by the number of students who came in to ask my opinions on abortion, drinking, and relationships with parents.

One night I was called in to help a family in which the father and son were having problems. That particular night the son, Alan, had been impatiently waiting for his dad to arrive with the family car. Alan was furious because he really needed the car. What he didn't know was his dad had just received bad news about the health of Alan's grandfather. Both Alan and his dad were upset, and they had a terrible argument when Alan's dad showed up late.

As I drove to Alan's, I thought, *Why did they call me? I feel as if I just jumped off the high dive. They're going to expect me to come up with some solutions and answers, and I don't know what I'm going to say!* When I got to Alan's house, the three of us talked, prayed together, and eventually worked out the problems. One of the things I had to learn quickly was to listen and then help students and their parents clear up the fog of their clouded thinking. In the eyes of the students I had become an instant expert on problems and a role model for all relationships.

Another time, a girl came into my office and talked about the sexual abuse in her family. I had never counseled a student with that sort of experience before. It was news to me that part of my job would be to solve those kinds of problems. During my first year at Walnut Creek, I was called several times to go to the youth home to pick up kids who had been arrested for drugs or for stealing cars. These were all new experiences for me, but working through each of them helped me to gain self-confidence.

The role model pressures were especially difficult to handle. I had to resist giving academic replies to students when they expected me to have instant answers. These pressures, combined with the "messiah mentality" pressures, caused me to expect students to listen to me. After all the years of effort and money I had put into becoming a seminary graduate, it seemed they should listen to me because of the authority of my background. However, I began to realize eventually that students weren't responding to my great wisdom, but to my position and circumstances. I realize now that instead of giving instant answers, I should have listened to students and helped them discover the answers for themselves.

Another limited perspective I had in my Walnut Creek ministry was my obsession with becoming a pastor—or at least being treated as a pastor. Maybe this sounds inconsistent with my frustrations over the pressures of "messiah mentality" and role modeling, but I strongly wanted people to perceive me as a full-fledged pastor. Getting licensed, going through ordination, performing weddings and funerals, being on the platform—these were all important goals. I wanted to be seen in a pastoral role, not just as the "kid who works with the high school students."

I would inwardly flinch when introduced as the youth *director* instead of the youth *pastor*. Somehow the term *director* implied programming to me and the word *pastor* implied ministry, on which I place a higher value. It still bothers me—and other youth ministry professionals—to feel degraded because we've given our lives to students.

BUILDING SELF-CONFIDENCE
During my first year at the Walnut Creek church, I discovered several ways to build self-confidence while trying to avoid the "messiah mentality." I became more confident in my ministry as I

realized that it is *God's work* to disciple students through me—not *my work* to disciple students through God.

Trying to make it *my work* instead of *God's work* just led to frustration and a constant search for instant success. I got angry when I worked hard planning an event, and kids did not come because their friends didn't come, or because it was something new and they didn't want to try it. For example, the students had a tradition of holding their winter retreat at Hume Lake, a large Christian conference center. The problem was that our small group of 40 or 50 kids got lost when they camped with another 450 high school students. So I said, "Why don't we take our own winter retreat. We'll rent a camp, get our own speaker, bring our own music, and have a better experience." The kids really rebelled about a change in location. Even though I felt it would be better for them to get to know each other, they wanted the large group experience. I responded with anger, and pride crept into my life when I could not get the responses I was told in seminary that I should get.

I overcame the "messiah mentality" and gained self-confidence as I began to see my programming as a vehicle through which God can work. When a kid doesn't relate to my youth program, it may be the kid's problem. When the kid doesn't relate to God, it's my

SURE, NO PROBLEM!

job as youth pastor to provide stimuli to bring that student closer to God.

I discovered that I'm not always the best person for a certain job. For instance, some of the students enjoyed horseback riding, so I recruited Ken Stuckey as an intern. Ken was a race car mechanic who wore cowboy boots and blue jeans, talked a little bit earthy, and drove an old pickup truck. He was more into expository teaching while I used a topical approach. We found that a whole group of students related far better to him than to me. For a while, that bothered me, but I soon discovered that this group of students was more sociologically comfortable with Ken and therefore more spiritually open.

During my first year at Walnut Creek, my self-confidence increased as I built a staff of supportive adults around me who wanted to share the ministry. When Jesus walked by the Sea of Galilee, we're told that He called to the fishermen, "Come, follow Me, and I will make you fishers of men" (Mark 1:17). He doesn't say, "Come *and* follow." He implies, "You come, follow, and then you do the same things that I am doing!" In the same way, as I build a staff, I increase the amount and quality of "fishing" (ministry) that my program can produce because of the varied personalities involved.

While youth pastors are often scheduled to work with the whole youth program, and equipped to work for the whole youth ministry, they are gifted with specific ministries to certain kids. If students at Walnut Creek didn't respond to my personality or gifts, then I provided them with adults to whom they could relate.

Another way I built self-confidence was by being intentional—keeping in mind the specific purpose of each activity. As I got caught up in the messiah mentality, I went off on tangents to meet all the specific needs of different individuals. Some of the students were very basketball-oriented. I enjoyed playing basketball, so I created a league for my students and refereed all the games. It took three nights out of every week. But after a basketball game, whom do you hate? The referee. There were all kinds of people who could referee the games, but I felt as if I was expected to be there. Instead of building relationships, my striped referee's shirt created a roadblock to meeting students, and this activity lost its original intent.

While spreading myself so thin, I really struggled with my personal walk with God. My devotions and love for God were suddenly replaced by my hours of preparation to meet the various needs of students. I spent my quiet time with God preparing my next Bible study. The Bible became a *tool* for ministry rather than the Word of God for Ridge Burns' life.

My struggles with a devotional life were resolved as I committed myself to learning how to *act* instead of *react*. Each morning I spent time alone with God in the church sanctuary. Before going to my office, I reviewed the day and a portion of God's Word to prepare myself for ministry. As I discovered the futility of tangents, I learned to plan my days by being intentional about what I did, instead of simply trying to extinguish the fires that surrounded me.

Finally, I discovered that waiting for God's timing builds self-confidence in ministry. The successful youth pastor is the one who has the right idea at the right time with the right students. In Acts 3, we're told that Peter healed a man crippled from birth. In verse 2, we find that the man was carried to the temple gate every day to beg. The key words are "every day." Jesus had walked through that gate many times during His ministry. He probably saw that crippled man, and yet He wasn't compelled to heal him. Why? It would have been a good act, but the wrong timing. In some way, that crippled man was reserved for Peter and John's ministry and that day is recorded in Acts 3:1-11.

If I am unable to minister to a student, I take great comfort from the fact that God will provide another person to meet that student's needs. In the same way, I have learned that there are people whom God is preserving for my ministry. And there are other people to whom I can minister even though I do not feel equipped to meet their needs. God has a timing for each person, and I need to be obedient to that timing. As I learn to depend on God's timing and daily commit my ministry to Him, I can be confident that "He who began a good work . . . will carry it on to completion" (Philippians 1:6).

SAMPLE JOB DESCRIPTION

A clearcut job description is vitally important to a youth pastor, as stated in chapter 2. Following is a sample job description that shows specific duties, responsibilities, requirements, and qualifications for a youth pastor.

I. Overall statement of responsibility
   A. Report to the senior pastor
   B. Oversee the junior high ministry
   C. Pastor and oversee the high school ministry
   D. Serve on the senior staff of the church and contribute to the establishment of strategy, philosophy, and direction of the overall church

II. Specific duties and responsibilities and weight of each

Hours	Weight	Responsibilities
15	25%	Speaking, teaching, and training speakers
1	2%	Planning themes and topics and providing focus for drama, media, and music
7	12%	Recruiting and training staff
3	5%	Administration
2	3%	Counseling parents/students
10	17%	Discipleship
5	8%	Campus ministry/evangelism
3	5%	Student leadership training
3	5%	Establishing general philosophy and the direction of the ministry—prayer, vision, planning, and evaluation
3	5%	Attending camps, retreats, special activities, big events; development of local and world outreach
2.5	4%	Working with elders, church staff, and other general church related work
2.5	4%	Junior high ministry
3	5%	Continuing education
60	**100%**	**TOTAL**

III. Minimum qualifications
  A. Master's degree
  B. Solid experience
  C. Qualities
    1. Personal qualities—loyal, team man, faithful, available, teachable, persevering, loves students, positive
    2. Spiritual qualities—filled with the Holy Spirit, has established an effective prayer life and Bible study habits, has a heart for God, meets qualifications of an elder in 1 Timothy 3 and Titus 1
    3. Leadership qualifications—people person, good manager, good communicator, visionary, and energetic.

SMALL CHURCH SPOTLIGHT

RIDGE: Pam, how do you deal with problems of self-confidence in a small church setting?

PAM: I think it's harder to build self-confidence at a small church than at a large church like yours. In your church, there's a lot of respect for the youth pastor's position. If you say, "Folks, we're all going to dress up as *wasteoids*. Let's put on white clothes and wear aluminum foil all night," all your students will probably say, "That's a great idea, Ridge!" If I tell my 8 or 10 students the same thing, they would all look at me like I was crazy, and say, "We're not going to do that!" There is power in numbers.

RIDGE: It seems to me the volunteer or lay youth worker in a small church needs to build credibility into his position because it isn't given to him by virtue of his position. I became youth pastor at my current church when I walked in the door. A volunteer in a small church may not become "youth pastor" until six months after he takes over the job. It's more of an earned position.
   What kind of related problems do you have with the "messiah mentality" in a small church?

PAM: I think the expectations that go along with the "messiah mentality" are less intense in a small church. Most parents don't have high expectations for me to meet their students' needs because I'm only considered a part-time person. But one of the problems with being a part-time youth worker is that parents view my job as scheduling and programming. If I plan enough parties, Bible studies, and special events, I have a successful youth program. Sometimes I have trouble remembering that it's not how many programs I plan that makes a successful youth ministry. Rather, it's how I contact and disciple students.

RIDGE: In some ways I envy you. If a kid isn't ministered to at a church of 2,000 members, it's the youth pastor's problem. If a kid isn't ministered to at your church of 50 members, it may be because you have another job. A volunteer always has the other part of his life as an excuse.

PAM: I still face a lot of criticism. In your church, parents get lost in the crowd, and you may only face their complaints at quarterly or annual parents' meetings. In my small church with fewer parents and kids, I may be confronted every Sunday morning by the parent sitting next to me. **Got any ideas on how to deal with weekly confrontations with parents?**

RIDGE: One of the principles of ministry that goes across any size group is one-to-one contact. If you only have nine or ten kids in your group, you should be able to spend time with those kids, call them, and monitor their activities sufficiently to please parents. Repetitious contact with students and parents can change their perceptions of you, and maybe even change their perceptions of your role.

PAM: Do you have any suggestions on how a new volunteer in youth ministry can build his self-confidence?

RIDGE: A new volunteer can write down realistic goals for what he can do. He should assess his time commitment and determine how many hours he can put into ministry. If he has ten hours a week, he can realistically decide how to spend those ten hours. Too often lay people don't assess the parameters of the job, and they self-destruct on tangents. Or they build a youth ministry that they can't handle with their limited time commitments. And tangents along with unrealistic goals and overcommitment destroy the volunteer's self-confidence.

PAM: A new volunteer can also recruit a staff so that his personality isn't the only one that influences his small group of kids. By having several other adults work with my youth group, I hope I'll be perceived as a delegator as well as the leader of the group. Then I can get more done in less time and increase my self-confidence.

RIDGE: Another way *all* youth workers can increase their self-confidence is through increased study of the Word of God. I try to go into my ministry fired up because I've spent some time in the Word, and God is alive in my life.

CREATE IN ME
ACCOUNTABILITY

THURSDAY, November 3
Tonight I went to my first Christian education committee meeting. I walked into the room and found a table full of people. There was a young woman with a degree in Christian education, the mother of a teenager, a school administrator, a financial consultant, and an elder.

The evening started off shakily. I was very nervous because I've never worked with a CE committee before. As I listened to committee members discuss business, I thought, "What if nobody here understands what it means to be on the cutting edge of youth ministry? Yet this is the group from whom I will have to get approval for my ministry decisions." I was feeling lonely and frustrated—that it was me against the entire committee.

But as the meeting continued, I saw that the committee members were trying to be very friendly. They told me what the youth group was like, its strengths and weaknesses, the history of the church, their hopes and dreams. I finally realized that the only thing they wanted me to do was to tell them what I was going to do.

I decided to share the results of my student survey with the committee. When they saw the results of the survey, they said, "Hey, this guy is a listener. We need to make some changes to have an effective youth ministry." I am so relieved! It looks as if we're going to be able to work as partners in youth ministry.

ACADEMIC INSTITUTIONS have built-in accountability structures in the traditional forms of grades and classes. A teacher hands out a syllabus, and if a student neglects assignments in that syllabus, he will receive low grades. When a student gets out of seminary and

53

enters the ministry, he has a choice. He can decide to be a lone ranger, do his own thing, and not be accountable to anyone. Or he can learn to develop his own accountability structures to God, the church, the students, and their parents.

In this chapter, I have tried to show how accountability and priorities mesh. Priorities work themselves out through accountability. For example, the only way for me to make my wife and family a priority is to have some sort of accountability to them. I have to allow my family to tell me when I am not giving them enough quality time.

Accountability is important as a way to keep me going in the right direction. Without accountability I'm off on tangents, false doctrines, or even false programming. My journal entry of that first Christian education committee meeting is just one example of how expectations and accountability became important issues in my ministry.

During that year I suffered some hard criticism. I was very tired physically—I found myself falling asleep in my office or in church after speaking on Sunday morning. And I began to lose students to other ministries. It was also the year I discovered that Christian education committee members, parents, and even senior pastors have hidden agendas regarding youth ministry. By hidden agendas, I mean unwritten or unspoken expectations concerning the role of an effective youth pastor. Because they are unwritten and unspoken agendas, a youth pastor may not realize that his success is going to be measured by how he meets those goals.

COMMITTEE AGENDAS

One of my surprises in youth ministry came in regard to the committee structure at the Evangelical Free Church of Walnut Creek. The Christian education committee was responsible for all components of ministry for children, junior highers, high schoolers, college students, and adults.

As I look back on that committee, I realize that each member was carrying around expectations based on his experiences. The young woman with a degree in Christian education was anxious to impress me with her knowledge and skills; the mother was upset that her son was not being ministered to by the church; the school administrator was concerned about behavioral objectives; the financial whiz was primarily concerned with fiscal accountability; and the elder's main agenda was to keep peace in the "family."

There were several ways that these people's hidden agendas

affected committee meetings. If the son of one of the committee members was particularly gifted in music and my youth program was not meeting that young man's need, there was a tendency on that committee member's part to evaluate the whole program based on a weakness in music. I never realized how subjective the evaluation process could be.

Another hidden agenda surfaced in regard to the fact that our church was part of a small denomination, the Evangelical Free Church of America, which has a youth program called Free Church Youth Fellowship (FCYF). The Free Church is headquartered in Minneapolis, Minnesota, and northern California kids had a hard time relating to denominational events that had a Midwestern flavor. Some of the committee members, who came from a long-term mainline Free Church background, wanted me to be a traditional Free Church youth pastor. This meant they expected me to participate in Bible quizzing, national conferences, and camps run by the Free Church. For example, in the past, kids had memorized the Book of John and entered national Free Church quiz competitions. This was just not my style! So when I suggested running my own conferences and camps, I met with some resistance. Once I learned that the committee was primarily concerned that our

HEY, THE YOUTH PASTOR SAID WE COULD USE THE GYM.

church kids were not going to have fellowship with other Free Church kids, I began involving the Free Churches from our western district in my own programs. Running camps and conferences in this way helped the denomination, preserved my style, and cut through some of the committee members' resistance.

After I had been at Walnut Creek for several months, I came to the CE committee with a decision that was going to cost them some money: I wanted to redecorate the junior high Sunday School room. It was important to give junior high students a place to call their own because the high school programs had always been given priority. The junior high group was currently meeting in the old high school room which had not been redecorated in years. The room—40 or 50 feet long and about 15 feet wide—had high ceilings, institutional green walls, indoor/outdoor carpeting with too much red punch spilled on it, and mismatched chairs. I had asked a decorator to make suggestions on how to make the room more educationally sound. Naively, I thought my 10-minute report, along with the decorator's suggestions, would meet with quick approval. I had no idea that this project would be delayed for three months because the CE committee couldn't come to a consensus on funding, time schedules, and the color and grade of the carpeting.

Presenting my report, I was pumped. In my mind, I had the color schemes down, as well as the prices; I had everything bought and painted before I went into the meeting. About halfway through the proposal, I saw a few people getting uneasy. One man began nervously doodling on some paper while another lady didn't put down her cross-stitch all evening. I had expected these people to get excited about this proposal and say, "Let's go!" Instead they responded with questions like, "Have you checked the paint prices with Mr. Smith? He saved me eight cents a bucket when I painted my house." I couldn't seem to generate much enthusiasm for the proposal.

I was disappointed. The kids had gotten excited the moment I revealed the paint chips. They were ready to paint the walls that night. Adults didn't work that way.

As discussions continued, I began to feel as if the committee members were more interested in making sure their opinions were heard than in trying to understand the urgency of redecorating the classroom. I wanted them to listen to me and at my command, unanimously raise their hands and say, "Yes, Ridge, we see your point. Let's take care of this right away!" I left the meeting feeling like they had missed the whole point. I wasn't asking for a decorating committee—I was asking the committee to say, "Yeah, we believe in junior high school students, and we want to make sure that church facilities are conducive to ministry."

As I look back at this project, I realize that I was and still am wrong to expect committees to act with the urgency that I feel toward specific projects. My impatience has carried through all my ministry. I still feel as if the board of elders ought to say, "OK, Ridge, we'll get right on the problem." In this case, I never gave the committee a chance to figure out the problems with the junior high room and come to their own conclusions. I also could have put my report on paper and given it to committee members prior to the meeting. They would have been able to look at the information I had gathered and then check for themselves to see if they could get better prices.

The end of this story is that we put together a really nice room. But I had this vision that the painters would be there one day, the carpet layers the next, the people with the new blinds the next day, the cabinet maker would be in there—in one week we would do the whole thing. What I learned is that some guy in the church can always get cheap paint, some guy's got a carpet friend, and it always takes a long time to get things done.

Ultimately, it was an authority problem. This was the first battle in which I came to grips with the question, "Why should this committee slow me down? I've got everything figured out." Part of the reason that the committee slowed me down was because it was necessary to slow me down.

I forgot that these people did not live at the church as I did. They didn't have energy invested in my ministries and they didn't see students every day. Committee members had their own jobs and set of agendas. I could have accomplished a lot more if I had realized that when they came to meetings they needed time to shift from their personal agendas and warm up to the problems of church life.

PARENTAL AGENDAS

Not only was I accountable to the Christian education committee—I had to deal with parents' expectations. Youth pastors are sometimes caught between parents and kids. I found that I couldn't identify myself too closely with either group. Part of the reason I was accountable for parents' expectations of how to minister to their kids was that they viewed my role as bringing them closer together with their kids. Parents had expectations, and kids often manipulated their parents with me in the middle.

Every three or four months I called parents' meetings to inform them of the ministry programs I was planning. I was always amazed at the intensity of their questions. "Are we going to have a full-scale high school choir program started by this fall?" "My son thinks that Sunday School is boring. What are your qualifications for teachers?" One lady asked, "Do you ever ask kids to bring their Bibles to Sunday School, and if you do, do they ever use them?" It was obvious that her kid never brought his Bible because he was cutting Sunday School.

One of the most awkward situations I was faced with came when two parents quizzed me about the lack of music in the Sunday School program. Embarrassed because I didn't know their son, I tried to answer the questions graciously and as generally as possible. After the meeting I went back to look at the attendance records

PLANNING PARENTS' MEETINGS

Keep the following suggestions in mind when planning parents' meetings.

1. Set up a specific time and place where you can have some kind of social gathering prior to the meeting. Many of your parents' questions will be answered during that informal time when parents are talking and mingling with each other.

2. Keep the discussion directed toward the issues that are important. It's not a good idea to have an open-ended question and answer time. Go through one aspect of your program, tell the parents what you are doing, and then ask if there are any questions regarding that aspect.

3. Allow parents to help their young people at these meetings. Most parents come with a question about how the youth pastor is relating to their son or daughter. Therefore, as parents arrive, have them fill out questionnaires about their children. On the questionnaire ask, "How can I have a better ministry to your son or daughter?" In this way, the parents will feel they have an open route for giving suggestions regarding their personal agendas.

and discovered that this couple's son had not been attending Sunday School. Apparently, he had been cutting Sunday School class and living a lie at home in front of his parents. Again, the success or failure of my entire youth program seemed to be based on each individual kid's involvement.

It was scary to think that a kid could go home from church on a Sunday morning and tell his mom, "I didn't like Sunday School." The mother then felt she had every right to make me accountable for her son's lack of involvement, even though he might have a good reason for not enjoying Sunday School. For instance, he might have been out drinking the night before and then felt the convicting power of the Holy Spirit in the class that Sunday morning.

It was very difficult for me to be accountable to people's personal agendas. It still is. In fact, sometimes it's impossible to find out other people's expectations, much less try to meet them. But what really bothers me is when people only let me know their expectations when I *don't* meet them.

During that year, Walnut Creek Public School District did not have a good high school music program. Unknown to me, some of the parents felt the church needed to meet the music education need of their children. However, these feelings were never articulated until the end of the year at a congregational meeting. I was angry and frustrated, wondering why I was constantly being evaluated on criteria about which I had no knowledge. And most of the criticism was unspoken but subtle.

In the case of the Rhodes family, the expectations were a little more obvious. One morning Mrs. Rhodes came into my office and pleaded with me to make her daughter the leader of that year's mission trip. "Debbie's a great girl," I told her. "She's smart, attractive, and has a good relationship with the Lord. But she's not a leader."

By the anger on Mrs. Rhodes' face, it was obvious I'd touched a nerve. How could I have violated the number one rule in youth ministry: Never tell parents something negative about their kid without being willing to be part of the solution.

I tried to bail myself out of the situation by explaining to Mrs. Rhodes that the only way to be a trip leader was to be chosen by the previous year's leadership. But I had already lost her. After this meeting, Mrs. Rhodes spent the next two years of her life trying to prove that I was wrong about her daughter's leadership potential. At each parents' meeting, Mrs. Rhodes would make sure I was aware of Debbie's most recent accomplishments. Debbie was the kind of daughter any mom would want to have. She was cute, she sang in church, she was a wonderful person. But the kids didn't respect her as a motivational leader. While I knew Debbie was a leader in certain campus events, I also knew there was a big difference between leading a mission trip for God and being a student leader in high school.

As the conflict escalated, Professor Rhodes made an appointment with me. At our Saturday morning meeting, he proceeded to tell me what a poor leader I was and why his daughter was one of the real leaders of the church. It was almost as if his kid should get preference because he was in church leadership. Again I unwisely tried to explain that Debbie was not a leader.

We never got past this conflict. Professor and Mrs. Rhodes decided that I did not understand Debbie, and as a result, we were not able to work together. Mrs. Rhodes went on a real guilt trip about her relationship to God and to me. She frequently began to write me letters of apology. Still, her letters were filled with innuendos and questions. It was a complex, confusing situation.

The case of Professor and Mrs. Rhodes is a situation I mishandled. How could I have been so brutally honest? One good thing though—I did protect the trip! On the other hand, I lost the support of Professor and Mrs. Rhodes and diminished my ministry to Debbie.

Why didn't I stop and think before saying something I was going to regret? When Mrs. Rhodes first came to see me, I should have listened, prayed, and spent some time with her instead of giving my opinion on her daughter's qualifications for leadership. I learned the lesson that you can win the battle but you may lose your people. It wasn't worth it.

PASTORAL AGENDAS

As a new youth pastor, I turned to my senior pastor, Chuck Wickman, for support. His support grew as we spent time together talking about ourselves as people, not pastors. I discovered Chuck's many expectations for me as a youth pastor as well as his desire that I be his confidant and resident idea man.

Chuck's agenda for me was to help me become a better youth pastor, and he expected me to live within the structures of the church. I had a tendency to go outside those structures. He also helped me honor my accountability to the board and build up the body by participating in existing church structures. For example, I was constantly in trouble with the sound committee—the guys who ran the microphones, tape recorders, and the sound board. Many times I wanted to use the equipment in a nontraditional way, so I borrowed the key to the sound room from the janitor and got a key made for easy access to the equipment. It was a time saver, and no one even knew when the equipment was gone. When Chuck found out what I was doing, he made me get rid of my key and go through the existing structure just like everybody else.

Feeling it was important for kids to attend worship service, Chuck expected me to get lots of kids there. It had been a problem because with the church's small sanctuary, the kids had a hard time getting a seat, and when it got crowded, they would skip. This was one expectation that put me in conflict with Chuck. I felt pressured to get kids into the service even though I wasn't sure the service was as relevant for them as it should have been.

Chuck also had expectations for me outside youth ministry. He forced me out of the youth pastor box to do some things that I did not especially want to do, such as preaching, presiding over meetings, and planning worship . Though I know many youth pastors want to preach, it was not one of my gifts. By forcing me to preach, Chuck helped me develop much-needed skills in sermon preparation and public speaking.

Another way that Chuck challenged me was in the area of problem solving. He once told me, "It's going to be neat, Ridge, to hear the 25 ideas you come up with to solve this problem. Even though 24 of them will never work." I appreciated the fact that my senior pastor was willing to sit through the 24 ideas that wouldn't work in order to grab on to the one that would fly.

During that year, our church had some problems with a school that was using our church facility. The church was a little more free-thinking than the school in terms of social behavior. To make a clear distinction between church and school, a separate board was formed for the school. Then, the church decided to rent space to the school, but not support it financially.

It soon became evident that the church and school needed to part ways. But many of the church families were school families, and they found it convenient to send their children to school at our church. And it would have been tough for the school to move since our facility was the best in town. One day the conflict escalated, and Chuck was very frustrated. He called a meeting of the school families and the church families.

Chuck asked me, along with the rest of the staff, to sit in on the meeting and answer questions. It was a role that I was not expected to be in as a youth pastor, but Chuck wanted me to be part of the solution to the school problem. As I sat at a table facing a large group of angry parents, I thought to myself, *This is a pretty hostile meeting. I've got nothing to say to these parents. I'm not really involved in this situation.* At the same time, I knew that Chuck was giving me a good education on how to handle a sticky situation. My thoughts went from *Why am I here?* to *I'm glad I'm here!*

AFFIRMATION

Affirmation is a key to fulfillment in ministry. In my own case, one source of affirmation was the Christian education committee whose members served as more than checkpoints for me. Occasionally, after receiving letters from parents whose students had been ministered to, they praised me for what I did well. They were very concerned about Sunday School, and their expectations helped me to make positive changes.

The subjectivity of the committee's evaluation process created in me a desire to have clear-cut goals and objectives. As a result, I wrote measurable goals for my ministry and had them approved by the finance and Christian education committees so that they would have an objective basis for the evaluation process. By having written and communicated goals, I was able to smoke out hidden expectations before they became part of the evaluation process.

Another source of affirmation came through my student program, which included a large group Sunday School class and Wednesday night ministry modules centered around drama, puppets, readers' theater, auto mechanics, rest home ministries, and other projects. An adult staff supervised the seven or eight modules that met for one hour on Wednesday nights followed by Bible study and prayer.

To help students learn the joy of saying thanks, we held an all-church, end-of-the-year spaghetti dinner expressing appreciation to the church. The meal was funded by the high school students who provided entertainment through performances and reports from the ministry modules.

The evening was fantastic. Over 500 people filled the church gym. I was so proud of our students and grateful that God had allowed me to help the students put together such a great evening. There was a warm, loving feeling in the room as the students were affirmed by a congregation that felt the students were finally doing something *for* them instead of *to* them.

As Chuck Wickman went to the platform to close the evening with prayer, he said: "Pastor Burns has expressed thank-yous to his staff and to his students, and we've seen a great model of ministry. But it would be wrong if we didn't express our appreciation to him." He asked me to join him on the platform, and as I began to weave my way through the tables, the people gave me a standing ovation.

Looking at those people applauding, emotionally overwhelmed,

MINISTRY MODULES

The philosophy behind ministry modules is to provide students with opportunities for creative expression based on their interests. The problem with some youth programs is that they usually focus on discipleship, evangelism, or choir. If a student doesn't fit into one of those categories, he might not find the program particularly appealing. By encouraging small groups of students to participate in modules such as auto mechanics, rest home ministries, and puppet teams, a youth pastor can broaden his student ministry. It also provides him with opportunities to augment church services with modules like puppet and drama teams.

The disadvantage of ministry modules is that they sometimes cause fragmentation within a group. Some modules and their leaders are better than others. Also, if they all meet on the same night, tension builds as students want to be involved in more than one module. By being aware of the potential problem areas, you can deal with them before they get out of hand and damage what could be a very successful program for ministry.

The diagram on page 65 shows how ministry modules are organized at Wheaton Bible Church. There are six areas of ministry in the high school department—communications, special events and parents, caring, Sunday morning ministries, hospitality, and missions. After developing a philosophy and clear-cut objectives for each area of ministry, you can produce modules in which students participate. For example, to give students an appreciation of fine arts in a Christian setting, you can have modules in the areas of drama, journalism, video, or music. Develop your own diagram based on your students' interests and creativity.

I realized I'd done something that had allowed the people to capture the dream of reaching students for Christ. Their applause and their smiles seemed to say, "Ridge, you're a good youth pastor. We're glad you came." Suddenly, all the parents' meetings, conferences, and committee meetings made a little more sense.

A third source of affirmation came from Bev and Jim Linman. During our first year at Walnut Creek, they shared their home, their van, and their friendship with Robanne and me. They were, and still are, a constant source of encouragement in our lives. Often I would find notes of encouragement like the following one on my car or desk:

> Dear Ridge:
> Thanks! It's really neat that God has brought you and Robanne into our lives at just the right time. We really appreciate your ministry to us.
>   In Him,
>   Jim and Bev Linman

The Linmans and other parents told me how they felt about the youth programs in which their students were involved. Generally, they were very affirmative. I remember one dad pulling me into the restroom during a church service to tell me how impressed his son was with my ministry, how appreciative he was of Robanne and me, and what my ministry had meant to his family.

DEVELOPING ACCOUNTABILITY
In my second year at the Walnut Creek church, I discovered several ways to develop accountability in order to cope with others' expectations of my ministry. A key step involves slowly building one area of ministry at a time. We find an example of this in Nehemiah 2–3. When Nehemiah returned to Jerusalem to rebuild the walls of the defenseless city, he delegated responsibility to about 40 key men for the reconstruction of about 45 sections of the wall. Each group slowly worked on its section of the wall, but Nehemiah was the only one who could see the big picture of rebuilding the entire wall. He earned credibility by setting goals and patiently delegating the work to be done. As he became more accountable to the people, they became more accountable to him.

Just as Nehemiah needed to be a self-starter, a youth pastor needs to be accountable to himself by setting goals and objectives. One of the things I did during this year was to take my week and

DRAMA
NEWSPAPER

WINTER RETREAT TASK FORCE
SUMMER CAMP TASK FORCE

THE STUDENT BODY

COMMUNICATIONS

To bring to the students an appreciation of fine arts used in a Christian setting. The coordinator of communications should provide opportunity for Christian expression within the Student Body in fine arts.

SPECIAL EVENTS AND PARENTS

To provide communication & feedback from the parents and to facilitate special events such as winter retreat & monthly large group socials for the Student Body.

MEXICO TRIP

SIDEWALK
SUNDAY
SCHOOL
LEADERSHIP

PROJECT
SERVE
LEADERSHIP

MISSIONS

To bring students to a point of decision concerning worldview. It is also the function of this position to show students the possibilities of Christian service available to them, both worldwide & home.

RIDGE BURNS

Director of high school ministries

CARING

To facilitate spiritual & social growth through small group experiences with the Student Body and to monitor & encourage core group leaders.

AUTO
MECHANICS

REST HOME
MINISTRIES

HOSPITALITY

To facilitate & encourage body life within the Student Body & create student leadership which will model hospitality.

SUNDAY MORNING MINISTRIES

To facilitate an educational environment on Sunday mornings with the Student Body which will foster spiritual growth & Christian fellowship.

SOCIALS TASK FORCE

MEDIA PRODUCTION
DRAMA
GREETERS & FOLLOW-UP

decide to spend a percentage of time in study, a percentage of time in contact work, and a percentage of time working as a staff member. Then I graphed those percentages out and blocked out time each week. I gave that graph to my secretary and she forced me to maintain a semblance of that schedule.

Some youth pastors are able to work within a stricter schedule. For example, I know one youth pastor who comes in to work at 8:00 A.M., but he won't take phone calls before 10:30 A.M. He tells his secretary not to allow any interruptions. During this two and a half hours, he studies and gets all his paperwork done. From 10:30 to 11:00 A.M. he meets with the people in his office structure. Then he has a free flow afternoon.

One way to meet others' expectations is to determine your own goals, and then, like Nehemiah, slowly educate others about expanded programs. Churches hate surprises. If I clue the board or CE committee in on my ideas and give them enough time to process them, I usually do OK. For example, when I first arrived at Walnut Creek, borrowed vans and cars were the primary sources of transportation. As the youth group grew, a need for church-owned vehicles grew. Rather than rushing in during my first few months of ministry with a proposal for purchasing buses or vans, I talked to the finance committee and continued renting vehicles. Eventually, the church got tired of paying the rental bills and slowly began to see the need I was expressing.

A second step in attaining accountability is to use delegation. My plowing ahead to build various areas of ministry resulted in overcommitment. I was running three basketball leagues, two mission projects, weekly Bible studies, ministry modules, and campus ministries. Personal time evaporated; even Robanne had trouble getting time with me. The job I had created was bigger than I was.

In Exodus 18 we read that Moses' father-in-law, Jethro, came to visit him to see what he was doing. Jethro was delighted to hear about all the good things the Lord had done for Israel. He spent a few days with Moses observing him working from morning until evening. When Jethro saw all that Moses was doing for the people, he said, "Why do you alone sit as judge? . . . What you are doing is not good. You and these people who come to you will only wear yourselves out. The work is too heavy for you; you cannot handle it alone" (Exodus 18:14, 17-18). So Jethro counseled Moses to set up a staff to handle small groups of people. In the same way, a youth pastor can develop accountability in himself and others by being willing to delegate responsibilities.

Listening to students, parents, and friends is another step in developing accountability. During this second year, I felt it was very important to tell people how *I* felt. When things didn't go right, I became angry inside, and my anger showed itself through defensiveness. I'd make defensive statements; I'd avoid looking at the other person—unwilling to take time to listen, explain, and communicate effectively. If I could relive that year, I would ask people how *they* felt. I would maintain good eye contact, and ask God to help me feel what the person is feeling. I realize now that Walnut Creek parents and committee members were not saying, "Do what we tell you to do"; they just wanted me to listen to how they felt. As long as they were listened to, they were satisfied.

Jesus gave us a good example of this in John 5 when He approached the man lying by the pool of Bethesda. A multitude of sick, blind, and lame people surrounded this pool that was supposed to have magical healing qualities for the first person who bathed when the water bubbled like a jacuzzi. This particular man was waiting for his turn to be the first one in the pool.

When Jesus looked at the multitude of sick people, He began to focus on one person. Instead of telling the man how he could be healed, He asked him a question: "Do you want to get well?" What a principle! Jesus knew that all the man had were excuses of why he couldn't get well, and that he needed to vocalize those excuses before his heart would be open to ministry.

Instead of telling people what we think they *ought* to know, we can ask them what they *need* to know and perform ministry. I wish I had asked Mrs. Rhodes how she felt about her daughter instead of telling her how I felt about Debbie. I also wish I had asked the CE committee how I could best accomplish ministry within the church instead of telling them how I planned to do it.

I also learned that the people who follow me as a youth pastor may not be the same people who follow other youth pastors. Debbie may have been developed as a tremendous leader under somebody else's ministry.

Finding a spiritual mentor is a fourth step in developing accountability. In my case, that person was my senior pastor, Chuck Wickman. One of the strongest biblical examples of a spiritual mentor is Barnabas. We read about him in Acts 9 after the account of Saul's conversion on the road to Damascus. Known for his ruthlessness, Saul had spent his life trying to destroy Christians. When Saul appeared to the disciples, they were all afraid of him, not believing that he was really a disciple. Barnabas—who was

FINDING A SPIRITUAL MENTOR

A youth pastor can minister in a more powerful way if he has a spiritual mentor. This friend can help him develop account-ability and a wider perspective of his ministry. Here are three suggestions for finding a spiritual mentor:

1. Ask God to give you a spritual friend who will make you accountable.
2. Look for people in your life who can provide you with a ministry of encouragement and accountability.
3. Take a risk. Share some things about your own life and spirit with another person. Tell him about your failures and where you need to improve. If you take that risk, God will allow you to share your deep feelings together.

called the "son of encouragement"—took hold of Saul and brought him to the disciples, vouching for the truth of his conversion. Like Saul, we all need somebody who believes in us, even when we have scathing reputations. Youth pastors must find somebody who will give them encouragement and help them break into the inner core of the church.

When I was installed at Walnut Creek, Chuck commented in his installation sermon that the congregation should allow me time to dream, think, and program so that I could give the church my very best, not leftovers. Eighteen months later, those statements seemed far away. I was so busy that I couldn't think about dreaming. At that point, I thought many times about quitting, wanting to scream, "Why can't people see that I have dreams and goals? I need time to develop them! I need relief!"

Part of my problem was due to the fact that I was accustomed to an academic calendar. Every summer, Thanksgiving, Christmas, and Easter was a break. But now there were no breaks. In fact, the very times when I was used to having less pressure, there were more demands from kids who were out of school.

I can understand why so many youth pastors burn out after a year and a half at a church. That far into my ministry I needed to make some changes and get out of the structure that I had created. Little did I know that the next year was going to be even harder.

As I brought my frustrations, resentment, and heartaches to Chuck, I discovered he was not only my boss, but he was my friend. Though we didn't spend a lot of time together socially, we shared a great deal of time in ministry. In some ways, I became almost a son to Chuck. He constantly affirmed me in my ministry with notes like this one:

Thank you for coming to Walnut Creek—for joining the best staff in the country. Thank you for encouraging me and my ministry by who you are and what you have done in our body. Thanks, Ridge.
Chuck

Chuck allowed me to think out loud and to even express my faults out loud. I was highly motivated to please him, and therefore highly motivated to work with the church and overcome my burnout symptoms.

The fifth step of developing accountability is to allow others to broaden your perspective about ministry. Just as Jethro helped Moses analyze his ministry with Israel, God brought some people into my life who were able to help me deal with my problems in ministry. Chuck Wickman once told me, "Don't take life quite so seriously." I'd get worked up over some little issue that really would not affect the kingdom of God or my ministry, and Chuck would encourage me to let things just roll off my back.

Occasionally, Robanne would say to me, "Why don't we take a walk or go out to dinner?" She knew there were times when I needed to diffuse my anger or else I would say things I didn't mean. Both Chuck and Robanne were extremely important to me at this point because they protected me from making verbal mistakes. Even today I need to listen to the clues God gives me that I am losing my accountability.

Don Thomas, the church treasurer, helped broaden my perspective of servanthood. In the first years of my ministry, the youth budget doubled and then tripled. Each monthly financial report usually showed that I was overspent. Don liked to say that the only page of the budget that he needed to print in red was mine. At the same time, he said to me, "Ridge, spending is a sign of ministry."

One time I forgot to order a check for a retreat payment. At midnight the night before the retreat, I realized I had not ordered the check. I called Don, woke him up, and asked him if he would write me a check. Fully expecting a lecture about my inability to manage funds, I heard Don asking me to come right out and pick up the check. When I arrived at his home, he handed me the check and said, "Ridge, my ministry is to help with the finances of the church, but I want you to know I'll be praying for you. Each check that I write reminds me to pray for your ministry."

As I drove home, I thought to myself, *That's the kind of servanthood I want in my ministry as well.* Fortunately, Chuck, Don, and Robanne helped me gain a broader perspective of my ministry so I didn't do irreparable damage. They were able to see me as a person with feelings, dreams, and goals. By being openly honest with me, they helped me develop accountability both in my personal life and in my ministry.

SMALL CHURCH SPOTLIGHT

RIDGE: How is a part-time youth worker or volunteer accountable in a small church?

PAM: In terms of accountability, there are fewer places to hide in a small church. The volunteer or part-time person needs to recognize that it's even more important for him to have clear-cut goals and a job description. Because there's less space to hide, it's going to be tough.

RIDGE: If I was a part-timer I would not take the job of "working with the kids." I would ask, "What does *working with the kids* mean—not in terms of how many hours a week but in terms of how many events?" Some good questions to ask the board or Christian education committee are: "What will it mean for me to be successful?" "What does a successful youth program look like?"

PAM: I think accountability can be developed in a small church in most of the ways you suggest in chapter 3. The most difficult principle for *me* to apply is that of finding a spiritual mentor. In a small church, the part-timer or volunteer is usually dependent on the pastor for spiritual guidance and direction. Unfortunately, my current church is without a pastor.

RIDGE: In that case, I'd suggest you talk with some youth workers from other churches and get some guidance from them. By sharing problems and dreams, you can still broaden your perspective of your ministry.

PAM: Like the discussions we've had about applying the principles in this book!

RIDGE: Do you think ministry modules work in a small church setting?

PAM: The module program is hard to do in a small church because it takes a number of kids to do each module. The more modules you have, the more kids you need. Music is one of the best modules that can provide unity for a small group. Fifteen kids can put together a good program of music, but 15 kids out of a group of 200 doesn't look too cool.

RIDGE: Another module that works well with a small group is puppetry.

PAM: Yes, kids realize they don't need public speaking skills to perform a good puppet show. These kinds of activities allow kids to broaden their own skills and ministry experiences.

four
CREATE IN ME
RESILIENCE

Dear Ridge,

I wasn't planning on writing but I just had to because you are unfair and rude and I have to tell you how I feel. I came to you with a problem that I still have. I don't fit the standard of the "Flock pets" like Keri, Delayne, Mark, and Lois. No one really cares. And don't give me the "We all care and we're all one in the body of Christ." That's a lie if ever I heard one. The Sunday School teachers don't even speak to me.

I needed help and you didn't give a d___. It's true. Ridge, you're too wrapped up with your miracles and appointments. You're always trying to change the city and saying, "We're going to do a miracle," but you're too busy for those of us with problems. I'm for miracles if you help *us* too. But you're ignoring me!

The Flock is the pits. Personally, I only go because I know it would hurt my mom if I quit. The kids are all so cold and judgmental. Don't you dare say "that's just the way *you* feel," because it's not. I'm tired of getting spiritual cliches every time I need help.

I don't know at this point if I'll be back. You can say "Come back for God, Sarah," but I'm beginning to wonder if there really is a God. If you care to acknowledge this, please do—yet I'm not counting on it because I'm not Delayne or Keri. Thanks for showing me the truth.

Sarah Peterson

Just received this note. I don't know what to do with Sarah. She wants my sole attention and undivided commitment. I don't know how much more criticism I can take. Everywhere I turn I hear negative things about my ministry. I'm beginning to resent Sarah and students like her who are not supportive of what I'm trying to do here at Walnut Creek.

I feel overworked too. I'm so tired of events and activities. I just want to sit down and rest for a while. Robanne and I aren't spending enough time together. Days off are a joke. I need help—someone who can encourage me and help me see my ministry in a new way.

RESILIENCE IS THE ABILITY to recover from or adjust easily to misfortune. In this chapter, I want to emphasize how I was able to deal with criticism by building resilience in my life and ministry.

When criticism creeps in, a youth pastor often loses his sense of joy in ministry. The hurt and pain become so intense that he tends to forget his hopes and dreams for students. Then Satan gets a foothold.

A youth pastor must be prepared to respond to valid criticism and cope with unfounded criticism. If he can persevere and do the things that bring him the greatest joy, then he will build resilience. Developing communication skills and open relationships can greatly increase his effectiveness and prevent criticism from crushing his spirit.

A CRITICAL YEAR

This year of ministry was my most painful to date. I had to learn how to react to pain and criticism. My relationship with Sarah Peterson is just one example of the hurt I experienced.

I met Sarah when I first came to Walnut Creek, and soon realized that she had special needs. She didn't always fit in. While the Walnut Creek church was made up of mostly upper middle-class/lower upper-class families, Sarah was from a blue-collar home, and right away I saw that she did not have a good relationship with her family. Her parents put some strong demands on her; Mrs. Peterson was very concerned about her relationship with her daughter and whether Sarah was meeting all her expectations. Sarah's parents were involved in marriage counseling, and I think Sarah had some insecurities based on the instability of her parents' marriage.

Wanting to minister to Sarah, I spent time with her after Bible studies and before Sunday School. I also met her for lunch at school, saw her at football games, and wrote her a lot of letters. I really believed I was making an impact in her life.

We had many conversations about her relationship with her parents. After one of our early talks, I received this letter.

Dear Ridge,

Hi, I just want to thank you for being so nice Sunday night. Thanks for offering to let me stay with you and Robanne. It's neat to know I've got friends when I'm down. I talked to my mom last night. We were screaming at each other and being perfectly honest. By the time we were finished, we were both crying and I found out how much my parents really love me. Again, thank you so much. I love you and Robanne.

In His name,

Sarah Peterson

Robanne and I tried to minister to Sarah in as many ways as possible. We put her in a small group in the Flock, our high school group. The Flock was divided into Folds which were small groups of five or six students committed to each other. I gave Sarah an excellent leader who made sure that she felt loved and cared for, and it seemed as if the more time we spent with her, the more positive changes we saw.

In December I received another note from Sarah:

Dear Ridge,

I would like to thank you for helping me so much. As this holiday season comes I realize how much closer I've come to my family and that you helped me do it all. If it weren't for you I don't know where I'd be. I've grown so much closer to my parents. I've finally realized that I am somebody. Thank you so very much.

Luv always,

Sarah Peterson

Sarah's Fold leader thought she was responding well to the other students. Sarah was now making conscious choices to change her life. Instead of joining the partying crowd after every football game, she was now spending time with kids from the Flock. Sarah didn't have the upper-middle-class status of many of the kids in the group, so I had been happy to pour my life into this person that no one else seemed to care about. Yet I couldn't fulfill all her expectations. The following note arrived in September shortly after Sarah's August letter mentioned in my diary.

Ridge,

Thanks for the great snub this morning. You made me feel great. Just to inform you—this was my last Sunday. At least in the Flock.

Sarah Peterson

When I received this note, I thought, *I've invested a lot of time, effort, money, and caring on Sarah, and look at the results! Why would a kid who I really put my life into turn on me? I guess I'm not the miracle worker I thought I was.* I was angry and felt as if I had lost a friend.

I'm not quite sure what triggered Sarah's negative response. I probably walked by her at church without saying "Hello." I've learned that my face is very expressive, and I can either motivate or hurt kids with my body language. When I'm really excited, my eyes light up. When I am listening to a kid, but not thinking about him, he can see right through me.

As I began to devote equal time to other kids, Sarah seemed to want more and more of my undivided attention. I was never able to resolve this situation. Eventually, Sarah disassociated herself from the youth program except for her Fold group. But I realized that I was doing some pulling out as well; there was only so much time I could give Sarah. Even though my relationship with her deteriorated, I was able to have a good ministry with Sarah's brother, Ken. Her family stayed at the church in spite of the discomfort of my strained relationship with Sarah.

ATTACK #1
The youth program grew, and more and more students joined the Flock. As the number of students grew to well over 100, criticism also grew.

One of the strongest evidences of dissatisfaction focused on the youth mission trip. Over the previous two years, I had taken kids to Mexico on the "Mexicali" program, associated with Azusa Pacific University, in which students work in a small church at Michoacan de o' Campo just 60 miles south of the border. An

Easter break program consisting of running Vacation Bible Schools and construction projects, Mexicali had proved to be an excellent experience. The more time we spent in the Mexicali valley, the more we fell in love with that little church. Our kids left their hearts there every year.

The first year I took 20 students. The next year I took 35. The third year, more than 60 students wanted to go. The first year's budget had increased by 500 percent and had now become a major financial burden for the Walnut Creek church. Questions began to surface. "Why do you have to take the kids so far away when there are people who need ministry right here in town? Why don't we invest the trip money in local missions? Why don't we just send the trip money down there, and let them hire nationals who can really help the situation?"

It was frustrating. I felt the church had no vision of the impact the Mexicali mission trip had on the lives and futures of the students. Mexicali wasn't just a missionary trip; it was a way to get students in touch with the third world. Sending money to the nationals would have been a very good thing to do purely for mission, but it wouldn't change the lives of students.

Something happens when students are ministering to orphans who just want to be sung to. It's a unique experience to play soccer with kids who want to play all day so they can have contact with North Americans. Nothing can replace the joy in students' lives when they attend an evening service where 20 or 30 Mexican high school students come to know Jesus Christ as their personal Saviour.

But I didn't sense the church had that vision. Their questions focused on why we were taking students down to Mexico when people needed help just a mile or two away. What a frustration it was when the Christian education committee along with the Board of Elders said, "Why don't you take 30 kids on the trip and leave the other 30 home? The 30 who stay home can pray for the 30 going on the trip and conduct another ministry here in the community."

How out of touch can the elders be to make this decision? I thought. I was furious, but I went along with it. The trip was organized in such a way that 30 students would go to Mexico and 30 students would stay home. The student leaders and I worked up our own criteria for a balance in sex and class. Then students filled out applications, and we selected 30 applicants, including a category of students that we felt would benefit from this trip more than others. Though my student leaders helped make recommendations and

STAYING IN TOUCH WITH YOUR BOARD

Here are at least eight ways to stay in touch with your Board of Elders:

1. Take each elder out to lunch on a regular basis.
2. Visit your elders at their jobs. They'll love showing you where they work as well as introducing you to their colleagues.
3. Rotate the elders through your normal prayer life. Pray for one a week, and tell him you are praying for him especially.
4. Bounce all ideas off your elders before putting them into action. Ask them what issues need to be covered at parents' meetings. Use them as a board of reference.
5. Invite an elder and his spouse over for dinner once a month.
6. Take a telephone survey of your elders. If there is a particular issue facing your youth group, get your elders' opinions.
7. Invite your elders to attend youth ministries meetings.
8. Introduce the elders to your students. Have them explain their leadership positions to your group, and have a time of affirmation with students praying for the board.

selections for the trip, the parents saw me alone as the primary decision-maker.

On February 20, I spoke during the Sunday School hour about supporting each other in the body of Christ. Then I read the names of those who were going on the Mexicali trip. After the 11:00 A.M. service, a student's father cornered me in the janitor's closet. For 20 minutes, he told me what a bad decision I had made and how insensitive the church was to his daughter. I couldn't believe his anger and wondered at one point if I was going to be beaten to death with a broom! It was a grim situation. But as he was screaming and yelling at me in the closet, I thought to myself, *He's right. We've made money and a balanced budget more important than ministering to students.*

I never realized my decision to leave students at home would have such a terrible impact. How stupid I was to believe that kids who desired to go on the mission field and serve God would not be hurt.

This particular decision brought all sorts of criticism my way. One student wrote me a letter.

Dear Ridge,

I wanted to write to you about how I felt and where I am coming from. Two months ago, I came to you with a problem. I was having trouble getting in with the Flock and I really wanted some Christian fellowship because I couldn't get it at my school. You said you weren't aware of this problem, but you would work on it.

A month passed and I really didn't see any change. Now, two months have gone by and I am still not as close with the group as I would like to be. I sent my application in for the Mexicali trip hoping that on this trip I could get real close to the group.

Then last Sunday morning you gave the criteria used in selecting the Mexicali group. One method involved choosing people who were not able to be a part of the group but wanted to be. I thought, *Oh, that's me! I must be on that list.* Then you read the list and I was so shocked that my name wasn't on it. It was almost like a slap in the face. Now for six weeks you and your Flock will be preparing to go to Mexico and guess who is left out again. I don't care how much you say, "Oh, you are a part of it," because I'm not. I want you to know how much you hurt a person who wants help.

Last Sunday you spoke about devoting time to people who have problems and following through till the problems are solved. When I heard you, I said to myself, *Why preach it, Ridge, if you can't live it!*

Ridge, I hope you take this letter with God's love, for it is written in love, not in bitterness.

In Christ,

Liz Jones

Liz was right. I *was* insensitive. But I was caught between what I thought the church was asking me to do and what I felt I had to do as a youth pastor, and the church won out.

ATTACK #2

As the youth program grew, some kids felt uncomfortable being in a group alive with God because they were spiritually dead. These students began to have pains concerning the youth group. The old crew of kids who had ownership of the program became frustrated when more and more kids began to attend youth activities. The old crew's power was threatened in the context of a large group. Most of their complaints were not based on fact or even appropriate perceptions. However, I was the object of their anger.

At the same time, parents continued to critique the entire program based on the involvement of the kids who happened to live with them. I got criticisms like "Ridge, you're not bringing the group along in Christ," and "Ridge, you're not helping Joan grow in the Lord."

Some parents refused to see the greater good of having more kids coming to the church and participating in ministry outreach. They couldn't understand why I could not be intimately involved with each kid. The Mexicali decision only helped to increase the tension.

THE FINAL AMBUSH

One particular incident almost put me out of youth ministry. In May, I was asked to meet with the Board of Elders. At that meeting I was asked to respond to the following letter.

Dear Elders,

After prayer and great thought on certain aspects of our church, we feel it important that we express our concerns to you. We do this in a spirit of love.

Our concerns are: Are we teaching the youth in the church to grow in the Lord, the importance of Bible study, individually and in groups, and the responsibility of those who have heard the Word? Are we giving our youth sufficient structured Bible study during the Sunday School hour and other times?

Two of our children are in the seventh grade and of Fish Factory age. We arranged weekly music lessons and other outside activities so our boys could attend the Wednesday night Fish Factory. Then we discovered that the Wednesday program had been discontinued. Many of the parents met with Ridge Burns and did not agree with his reasoning that he must be in attendance with the Fish Factory Wednesday nights. We admit that in December three meetings were held on Wednesday nights on a trial basis. However, we feel these meetings were ill-planned at the most inopportune time and were not advertised well enough for good participation.

Our suggestion: Wednesday nights need to be returned on the church calendar as all-family Bible study nights. ALL pastors of the church or other qualified teachers should be responsible for teaching the youth on this evening.

We believe any person in the church interested in Bible study should be encouraged and not discouraged. One of our children wanted to study with the Tuesday afternoon Fish Factory but could not expend an hour each Tuesday from his schedule only to have a good portion of that hour for sports events rather than Bible study. Two times he called Ridge to inquire the time of the Bible study. He was not told the time when the Bible study would begin, and both times he attended, he missed out on the Bible study.

I am certain Ridge had a motive in his decision not to tell him when the Bible study would be held—perhaps he felt our son should be there for the whole hour—but I believe Ridge is lacking in empathy and not looking at the complete goal of educating our youth in the Word.

Sincerely,

Mr. and Mrs. Wilkerson

The Wilkersons went on to list 10 other complaints in a detailed four-page letter. The letter had been photocopied and sent to every elder and every committee chairman, and was widely circulated to most of the parents in the church.

I can't begin to describe my anger at this letter. I walked into the elders' meeting feeling as if I could lose my job. All the feelings of insecurity I had overcome in my first year at Walnut Creek returned. I found myself biting my fingernails and trying to calm a nervous stomach.

Point by point, I resjponded to the letter's complaints. Starting with a review of my work with the Fish Factory, our junior high youth group, I then shared a survey I had done with junior high students revealing that Wednesday night was not a good time for Fish Factory. Many students were used as baby-sitters to support the other ministries at the church on Wednesday evenings while other students had school commitments.

I explained to the elders that I did indeed meet with the Wilkersons to discuss the schedule change of the Fish Factory. However, the "many parents" mentioned in the letter who met with me were only four people. I described how I had tried to be as sensitive as possible to these four people. Perhaps I wasn't communicating as well as I could or should, I explained, but I certainly was trying to do the best I could to meet all the students' needs.

After I offered a detailed explanation of the issues in the letter, it didn't take long to realize that the elders were in my corner. My actions had been reasonable. Furthermore, the Wilkersons had diluted their criticism of the youth program by attacking at least 10 other areas of the church and its administration. As soon as I saw that the elders were going to be supportive, I was able to overcome my temporary lack of confidence, and left the meeting reassured.

BURNOUT
The Wilkerson letter brought one of the major criticisms in my ministry. Satan seemed to be gripping me with all kinds of critical letters and phone calls. Students began accusing me of favoritism as I became more and more defensive.

Emotionally, I was drained from work. Spiritually, I was defensive and critical toward the church. Physically, I was hurting due to an injury to my knee which resulted in the first surgery of my life.

Relationally, I was too busy to spend time with Robanne, who was teaching at the church's preschool and involved with ministry to some of the students in the youth group. My working relationship with my secretary was not strong. I had gotten into the habit of giving her vague instructions and information, and then making myself inaccessible to clarify my messages. My relationships with many of the students were deteriorating. I resented the students who were not supporting me appropriately and clung to those who supported me fully. This only fed the whole idea that I played favorites. I really felt as if Satan was working overtime on me. I was saturated, almost burned out.

One of my main frustrations during this difficult year of ministry was: *Why can't people understand that I'm a person with feelings too?* Parents would criticize the youth program in large group meetings, but they wouldn't make an appointment to discuss their complaints with me. There were simple answers to their questions, but I couldn't seem to get anywhere with them.

Church members didn't seem to understand that Robanne and I were still working on our marriage and that we had certain time demands. Though they were used to having a youth pastor, they weren't aware of the unfulfilled expectations they placed on me.

As criticisms poured in from parents and students, I began to recognize my limitations. *Perhaps I'm where God wants me to be*, I thought. *Maybe He wants me to come to a point where I don't want to do my job unless He goes before me.*

FAVORITISM

Under attack, I found it difficult to resist clinging to students who were very supportive. To counteract the accusations that I had favorites, I tried to put a student in leadership who was not a natural leader. For example, I made sure that the Flock's winter retreat was led by a new student in the group. Traditionally, longevity in the church had been a requirement for leadership. When I put a student who had just moved to Walnut Creek in a leadership role, kids' presuppositions were blown away.

I discovered that the accusation of playing favorites is part of youth ministry. Jesus probably had that criticism leveled at his relationships with Peter, James, and John. I can just imagine the rest of the disciples being jealous of these three men who witnessed the Transfiguration. I have often tried to put myself in the shoes of a disciple who was not one of those three men on the mountain. As a result, I've learned the hard way that I need to be open to new relationships in my life rather than clinging to students who can manipulate me with good words.

PAIN AND OVERCOMMITMENT

As my life throbbed with emotional, spiritual, and physical pain, I looked to God to supply me with a friend. I assumed that person would be another youth pastor or adult, but the Lord sent me a student.

Delayne Roethe was the 16-year-old daughter of a Navy captain. People noticed when this natural leader entered the room; Delayne was strong emotionally, physically, and spiritually. And she was willing to share her life with others. She arrived in Walnut Creek after spending the past two years living on a Navy base in Korea. Because she had moved so many times, Delayne understood what it meant to break into youth group cliques, and she closely identified with students who felt left out of the Flock.

I asked Delayne if she would give up going to Mexicali in exchange for the opportunity to run a ministry with those students who were not chosen for the mission trip. In February, she became the leader of what was called The Other Half. Her first task involved forming a prayer partner base where church families and students could sign up to pray for a student while he or she was in Mexicali.

At the same time, Delayne began to take on all kinds of criticism and turn it into emotional energy to change the lives of students. A student would say to her, "Ridge didn't select me for Mexicali." Delayne would give that kid a job in The Other Half. She helped plan a dinner for the Mexicali students and began to turn The Other Half's anger into joy.

When we returned from Mexico, the parking lot of the Walnut Creek church was decorated with "Welcome Home" banners. We were greeted by a large group of parents, and a dinner sponsored by The Other Half. This wonderful reception had been organized by Delayne.

I didn't realize that God was going to use a student to teach me how to deal with criticism and the pressures of youth ministry, but God gave me Delayne. He put her in my life to protect me from overcommitment and to rekindle my dreams of ministry. For example, Delayne had a dream for discipleship so we created a conference called *Walk This Way*. Over 1,000 students came to our church to learn about discipleship.

As my friendship with Delayne grew spiritually, I was able to

THE IMPACT OF SHORT-TERM MISSIONS

Short-term missions projects are defined as cross-cultural mission trips (either at domestic or foreign sites) that take place during school vacations, lasting one to eight weeks in duration. Short-term missionary projects have been viewed as an educational process to allow a student to evaluate his values and life's direction. It is particularly important to provide these opportunities at the high school level because high school students are very pliable and just beginning to formulate values.

There are three reasons why a church should become involved in short-term mission projects. The first reason is *education*. I don't expect students to become missionaries as a result of these trips. Rather, I want them to get acquainted with the mission process. Churches must realize that mission trips do not become an end in themselves; they merely feed the spiritual appetite of students so that some can begin planning to become career missionaries. I try to plan mission trips at the high school level so students will be able to more appropriately select colleges and curriculum to fulfill their mission goals.

The second reason churches should become involved in short-term missions is the benefit of *entry-level missions experiences for students*. Short-term missions projects that are appropriately designed can be the first real mission experiences for young people—giving them exposure to missions and getting them thinking about outreach ministry.

Churches should also be involved in short-term missions because these missions give students *opportunities to express their faith*. Too many times our programs are designed to teach students *about* their faith instead of providing opportunities for them to *express* their faith. The genius of short-term mission projects is that students are forced to articulate their faith and live in the context of another culture. To do this, a student must reevaluate his own culture and lifestyle to see if they are inconsistent with his stated faith.

break the syndrome of self-pity and defensiveness that criticism brings. I began to see hurt, criticism, and pain as stimuli from God to continue in ministry. In God's plan, I needed Delayne's help.

Later on in her life, she would need mine.

ESTABLISHING RESILIENCE

In my third year of ministry at Walnut Creek, I discovered five ways to establish resilience as I faced criticism. The first method is to *avoid sin*. When Paul was in front of the Council of Jerusalem (Acts 15), he was criticized not only for his ministry but also for his ability to relate to people. However, he still brought joy to the brethren.

One aspect of avoiding sin involved watching my mouth so gossip wouldn't feed my own criticism. For example, when Mr. and Mrs. Wilkerson sent their letter to the elders, it would have been very easy for me to criticize the Wilkersons and their children. I could have gathered an army by making insinuations and innuendos in front of my strong supporters. But this response of backbiting and rumor spreading would only result in confusion and turmoil. A large-scale example of the power of rumor occurs in Acts 19 where we read about Demetrius and the silversmiths' attempt to destroy Paul's reputation by spreading rumors. Their words led to a riot. The whole assembly was in confusion—the majority of the people not even knowing why they had come together. In the same way, too much unfounded talk and criticism can result in a church environment of mistrust, confrontation, and confusion.

The second way to develop resilience is to *view criticism as a test*. God puts us through tests, and if we pass those tests, He lets us go on to another level of spiritual maturity. When the Children of Israel walked through the desert in Sinai, God made them take a longer route because of their disobedience and murmuring. If they had simply stayed with the task and kept their eyes on the call of being led to the Promised Land, they would have arrived there sooner. When I began to view criticism as a test, I became more obedient and in turn was able to overcome the pain of criticism.

A third method for building resilience is to *dream your way out of criticism*. I began to identify with Caleb and Joshua, two visionaries who truthfully reported on their reconnaissance mission into Canaan (Numbers 13–14). These two men were greeted with criticism and contempt, but rather than becoming discouraged, Caleb and Joshua persisted in their faith and remained true to their vision of the "land of milk and honey." As a result, their visions of Israel in Canaan became a reality 40 years later.

Criticism points me to the past or makes me a prisoner of the present. I have learned to escape the criticism trap by dreaming and motivating my students to go in a whole different direction than they have ever considered before. Dreaming also reduced my ability to be defensive. For instance, one of my strongest criticisms concerned students not being discipled. I began to think, *Maybe they aren't being discipled. Maybe I need to have a special conference on discipleship and watch the kids grow toward more maturity in Christ.* Therefore, out of criticism came the dream to bring 1,000 high school students together in order to change their lives for Christ.

Dreaming gave me a positive frame of reference. However, the dreams and visions of the students were often bigger than the dreams and visions of the church. My problem was I didn't take the time to integrate the high school program into the whole church. I could have taken an elder with me to Mexicali to see how hard the students worked. I could have allowed more parents to be involved in the youth program. By allowing other people to be my spokesmen, I could have helped the church understand our dreams and visions.

Fourthly, it's important to realize that *there is an element of truth to all criticism.* In Revelation 2:1-6, the church at Ephesus was criticized because in spite of a reputation for active programs, it was spiritually dead, having lost its foundational root of being in love with God. One of the letters I received during the year said that I lacked empathy and sensitivity to the goal of educating youth. There was an element of truth in that. I am not naturally empathic; that is, I don't naturally listen well to people with problems. I need to learn to develop that skill.

Finally, I discovered the best way to cope with criticism and establish resilience is to *build strong relationships with the senior pastor and the church.* I like what it says in Acts 2:14 about Peter and the Eleven standing up in defense of the Gospel. I could not have dealt with criticism without the solid support of Pastor Chuck Wickman, Delayne Roethe, and the Board of Elders.

One of the reasons the elders were so supportive of me was because I was open in my relationship with them. When Christ rebuked His disciples, His criticisms must have been more easily accepted because of the special relationships He had built with them. In the same way, I shared dreams and frustrations with the Board of Elders, investing time with each individual. Even though I wanted to react defensively to criticism, I tried to resist that temptation because of their spirit of support.

In fact, the elders would often humor me. It was fun to be with a group that was willing to commend me on doing a great job while

SHORT-TERM DREAMS

Taking students on mission trips is a dream. Some people may not understand that dream. Expect criticism as part of the educational process. Help your students work through criticism and accomplish the dream. The three most common dream killer statements are:

1. "There are needy people right here in our city. Why don't you do a project here? Why go so far away and spend money on people we don't even know?" There's an element of truth to this statement. Don't start a missions program by sending students overseas; start in your own city or high school. Build a sensitivity toward outreach in all areas of life. If you begin with the most dramatic programs, students respond to the travel and excitement of the different cultures, and not to the dream of expressing their Christian faith.

2. "It costs so much. Couldn't we just send them the money and let the missionaries we support use that money to accomplish the same things?" The people who give this kind of criticism don't understand that this is a missions *education* project. Don't pretend you're involved in total missions, but explain that you're trying to invest some money in students while they are impressionable so they may retain a concern for missions six or seven years down the road.

3. "My aunt is a missionary and she had some high school students come over for the summer and she said it was more bother than it was worth." Students who are inadequately trained can create problems and more work for the missionaries. Not all career missionaries can handle short-term missionaries. You have to be sure that the environment in which you are placing your students is the kind of environment that can handle the high-energy activity that high school students produce.

The most important thing to remember about short-term mission work is that it begins with a heart broken for the hurts of the world. You cannot take students further than you've been yourself.

still taking criticism seriously. They affirmed me verbally as well as through financial raises.

As criticism continues to be a part of my ministry, I am reminded of James 1:2-3: "Consider it pure joy, my brothers, whenever you face trials of many kinds, because you know that the testing of your faith develops perseverance." Criticism and persecution have produced endurance and smoothed my rough edges. When criticism has come, I've tried to remember that even youth pastors who appear to be successful are probably under the same fire of criticism. More importantly, the *absence* of criticism is not an indication of success, as I discovered in my next year at Walnut Creek.

PLANNING A MISSION TRIP

One way to schedule a trip is through a missions agency that specializes in taking groups of high school students. If your group is small enough, or if only five or six students are interested in a short-term mission project, you can run that project yourself. Following are some steps to help you plan a short-term mission trip.

Step 1—Share your vision with church and student leadership. Before sharing your vision with your pastor, mission board, or Christian education committee, develop a short mission statement that you will be able to use as a basis for your discussion. Get full, conceptual approval from your pastor, Christian education committee, and/or missions board before proceeding. It is equally important to share your vision with key student leaders. Get full conceptual approval from your youth group cabinet or leadership team before proceeding. Short-term mission projects require a high degree of student ownership. Omitting students from the planning process will cause problems for you later.

Step 2—Select a mission site. Your mission site is determined by your choice and structure of a project. One-third of the time should be spent in a physical project—structures that allow the local ministry to continue after students leave. Another third should be invested in a person-to-person ministry. Even in situations where students do not know the language and have to work through an interpreter, Vacation Bible Schools and backyard Bible clubs provide them with effective ways to articulate their faith on a one-to-one level. The last third should be invested in group building, making students feel like a team.

To select a site, contact your church-supported missionaries. Often they know of projects in their city or country with which you can help. International Teams in Prospect Heights, Illinois is a great resource for contacts on mission sites. Once the initial contact is made, establish who the site manager will be and stay in contact with that person on a regular basis. Several months prior to the trip, visit the site and make sure the site can actually accommodate your group.

Step 3—Secure adult sponsors. Try to establish adult sponsors at least four months before your trip. This helps the sponsors arrange their vacation schedules as well as providing time for training.

Step 4—Develop a budget. The greatest source of controversy for a short-term mission project is the cost. Ask the treasurer of your church to set up a budget and an accounting procedure for your particular trip. Fund-raising projects might include ideas such as a simulated refugee camp, a bicycle moto-cross, a concert series, servant days, as well as selling items to produce a profit.

Money is not your greatest obstacle—motivation is. If students are properly motivated, they will raise money for any project. If you need some good ideas on how to raise money, ask students who have raised money for their band uniforms, cheerleading camps, or other school activities. They're experts.

Step 5—Encourage total church involvement. The goal of a summer mission trip is to make it a total church experience. Though it seems easiest to leave on a Friday evening after adult sponsors get off work, try to schedule your departure after the Sunday morning worship service. Print a prayer card for each student so he can share with his friends and enlist prayer support. Set up a Prayer Partners program where church families can pray each day for a specific student while he is on the trip. Have your students write those Prayer Partners during their experience to give them a firsthand report.

Step 6—Provide adequate training. The most common complaint from missionaries about short-term mission projects is that we send ill-prepared, ill-trained students who provide more problems than help. The missionaries have a good point. Unless we are willing to put time and effort into training students, we have no business sending them into cross-cultural situations.

Begin your training with a very thorough application and interview process. Orientation should include a cross-cultural experience such as visiting an inner-city church if you are from a suburban church, or vice versa. Include such things as an obstacle course, Bible verse memorization, evangelism training, cultural training, and construction instruction to prepare students spiritually, physically, and socially. Mission organizations like TEAM, Greater Europe Mission, and International Teams can provide you with training materials.

Step 7—Follow up the trip to solidify the impact. Provide year-round opportunities to satisfy your students' appetites for missionary service. Be sure you don't compartmentalize missions into a two- or three-week summer approach. Provide your students with integrated activities to solidify the impact of their short-term trip.

SMALL CHURCH SPOTLIGHT

RIDGE: Pam, how do you deal with criticism in a small church setting?

PAM: When I feel overpowered by criticism, I usually share my frustrations with a friend who is involved in some part-time youth work at another church in the community. She understands my trials because she is also experiencing criticism.

RIDGE: At my church, I have like-minded staff members. I can go across the hall to the junior high youth pastor's office to talk. He understands parental criticism because he gets it too. He understands a kid who leaves the program because he is experiencing the same problems. If you're all by yourself, I think you need to find fellowship among other youth pastors or other volunteers in the area.

PAM: I try to schedule regular times to meet other part-timers who are like-minded even if they aren't part of my church, because they still feel the same things that I feel. You can find people like that at Sunday School conventions, one-day workshops, and youth conferences.

RIDGE: Or you could find a youth pastor who is full-time in the area and spend time with him. I think one of the things that's helped our relationship is that you can relate to what I'm talking about even though our groups are enormously different.

PAM: One thing about volunteers is that they don't have to put up with criticism. They can quit. They can say, "I get hacked off at work; why should I put up with this at church? Here I am serving the Lord for nothing!"

RIDGE: I would say to a volunteer, "That's part of ministry. That's part of God shaping you into what He wants you to be. He puts people in your life who may hurt you a little bit." Some kids may say things that may make a youth worker more sensitive to areas where he needs to be sensitive. Instead of giving up and running from criticism, we career youth pastors stay in ministry because we're "called."

PAM: If you're a volunteer, you are also called. But it seems to be an easier choice to leave that ministry position. **What kind of dreams can a volunteer or part-time person have?**

RIDGE: One of the dreams that a small-church volunteer can have, that I can't have as a large church pastor, is a personal relationship with every kid. If I only had 20 kids in my youth group, I could accomplish some big dreams by spending time with each kid. I could write an almost individualized curriculum program for those students.

I have a little core group of six guys. One of my dreams for them is to go on a small mission trip together. We're going to build a roof on a woman's house in downstate Illinois. So even this small group can accomplish something big.

PAM: There's a church in Westmont, Illinois that has a small youth group of 15 kids. They want to ride their bikes around Lake Michigan during the summer. And they're going to do puppet shows out of a van in the evenings in state parks. That's a big dream for a small youth group.

One of my dreams was to take my group to a youth conference in Colorado. I wanted to schedule some sort of service project for our church which was contributing financially to that trip. My students decided to volunteer their services to church members each Saturday for two months prior to the trip. They washed windows, mowed lawns, weeded gardens, and emptied water heaters. More important to me, they built relationships with many older church members and experienced the joy of really serving people in need.

CREATE IN ME
BROKENNESS

SUNDAY, March 3

I've been thinking about Anna. I remember when our mission team first arrived in Michoacan de o'Campo, Mexico. A mass of kids with balls and jump ropes stormed the van. In the midst of all the confusion, a little five-year-old girl named Anna came running up to me and sat on my lap. We talked and sang. From that time on we became inseparable.

The first three years that I took students to Mexicali, I spent most of my time gassing up vans, searching for puppets, and making sure curriculum, movie projectors, and the sound system were available. I'd never had time to make friends with the nationals. But this year was different. Anna just kept following me around, holding my hand. At first, I considered her a nuisance, but I finally realized God put her in my life in order to make me a little more sensitive to the ministry that my students were going through. I don't know why she chose me, but somehow, Anna was able to penetrate my heart.

Everytime I think of saying good-bye to her, I want to cry. I think I left a little bit of my heart with her in Mexico. She was a lovable little girl who was willing to spend a lot of time with me. I wonder what the Lord is doing in her life now and who she is becoming.

SOME YOUTH PASTORS can do youth ministry without God. With their highly professional techniques, skills, and talents, they are able to maintain their programs and produce temporary results in their students. But these youth pastors need to put themselves into situations where they can fail and experience brokenness.

Brokenness is a lack of pride. It's a position where God takes our pride, breaks us, and makes us more pliable and humble. Once we've been broken, He shows us that we must do ministry through His Spirit if we want to see lasting results in our students.

Everyone is broken or scarred by something. Some people are haunted by scars from alcohol, drugs, sex, or family relationships. But God is looking for people whose hearts have been broken and burdened for others. A youth pastor must allow God to put spiritual scars in his life that will haunt him and yet be good for him. By putting himself in the position of being scarred by God, a youth pastor can have a tender heart, sensitive to the needs of his students and staff.

In the first two years of my ministry, God used the scars of failure to keep me on my knees in prayer. Some of the criticism that I suffered during my third year at Walnut Creek was God building humility in me. In this chapter, I hope to show how my heart and ministry were broken and scarred by people who were hurting— Delayne, Anna, my Bible study group, boat people in Hong Kong, refugees in Thailand, lepers in India.

THE COMMUNITY
My first year of ministry at Walnut Creek had been a situation where I could do no wrong. My second year was filled with discovery and affirmation as programs began to solidify and stabilize. The third year was consumed with criticism concerning committees and structures. During the fourth year, I began to see the fruit of my work over the first three years. The youth program at Walnut Creek really began to be rewarding and successful as I saw kids come to know the Lord. The numbers were increasing more than ever before, even though I had taken much criticism during the previous year.

In the three years we had been at Walnut Creek, Robanne and I had begun to feel very isolated. Many of our contemporaries had started families and their lives were focused on their children. We began to drift away, isolating ourselves from our peers because their discussions of diapers, baby formulas, and Lamaze techniques at Sunday School and socials were not of interest to us. Also, our busy schedules were so wrapped up with students that we rarely attended any functions for our age-group. Our best friends became students and our only contacts with our peers were high school sponsors.

Feeling frustrated, we began a Bible study for our peers. In that Bible study were four couples. While we were all the same age, we were all very much different—a lawyer, a computer expert, a public

PORTLOK

**"HE'S GOING THROUGH A ROUGH TIME.
A STUDENT'S PET GOLDFISH DIED."**

relations person, two secretaries, a missionary, Robanne, and me. Our common base lay in the fact that we were childless couples who desired fellowship.

It was the kind of group that could sit around and talk about serious issues until 2:00 A.M. and yet still be able to laugh together. Robanne and I found ourselves really enjoying these people who shared our concerns and humor. For example, one weekend the eight of us decided to take a retreat at a summer home that belonged to one of the couple's parents. There were only two bedrooms in the house, so all the guys ended up in one bedroom with all the girls in the second room. During the evening, I had to go to the bathroom. I heard the commode flush on the top floor, and suddenly water poured all over the place. I was drenched! I could hear the rest of the group dying laughing. They had conveniently forgotten to tell me that if someone flushed the commode on the top floor, the one on the bottom floor exploded with water. We had a lot of fun.

We began to study Bonhoeffer's *Life Together*, a book written during World War II for a German school as a manual on Christian fellowship. Bonhoeffer's theory is that we need to do things that will corporately uplift Christ. During the weeks that followed, the group began considering an alternative living situation based on my understanding of the book. One night, in the middle of a discussion at the Bible study, I asked, "Why don't we try to live this out? Why don't we sell our houses or get out of our apartment leases and move into a contiguous housing situation. Let's see if we can find a condominium complex where we can buy adjacent apartments, eat common meals together, carpool, worship, and share our resources."

Robanne and I had bought a condominium, had a great mortgage interest rate, and weren't really interested in changing that. However, we felt it was important for us to find fellowship and do something distinctly different with our faith. So after a lot of thinking, prayer, and Bible study, we put our condominium up for sale, and the four couples began the search for a place where God would want this community to start. We had reevaluated our lives and decided to commit ourselves more fully to God and each other. One of our chief objectives was to demonstrate an alternative living style to the parents and students at the Walnut Creek church.

As a group we decided to share information about our salaries. At first, we avoided saying how much we made because we knew the salaries would indicate the amount of financial responsibility each couple would have. For example, because the lawyer had a much larger salary than the missionary, he would probably have to risk more money on this venture. We were all very tense on the night we shared our financial positions. But it helped us begin to break down the walls between us and gave us a sense of freedom.

It wasn't too long before the group found a small condominium complex that had four units that were for sale. Three of the couples were able to buy their own condos, but it was a miracle to see how God directed us in financing the fourth couple's place. The four couples entered into an agreement not only to buy their own homes, but to cosign for the financing of another one. It was a risky agreement, but it helped us affirm our commitment to each other. The financial problems were worked out and we were able to buy those units.

We met for prayer every week and became known as "The Community." It was sort of like living in a college dorm situation where there was easy accessibility to fellowship, but each couple was able to retain its privacy. There were many late-night talks. We'd stay up until all hours discussing theological matters or problems at the church. These discussions weren't gossip in a negative sense; they were conversations that helped us to better understand the church and dream about possibilities in ministry. I really began to love other people my own age the way that I loved high school students. It was exciting to see that the principles of spending time building relationships applied in my peer relationships as well as my youth ministry.

Our community lifestyle cut across the sociological strata of Walnut Creek. Walnut Creek is an upper middle class/lower upper class community. Hospitality and community feeling are strangers to this city. People build their houses, put up fences or large hedges, and stake their own claims, living somewhat in isolation. We four couples broke all the rules when we sold our homes in order to live closer to each other with open doors.

The church reacted in different ways to the Community. A few of the people thought what we were doing was almost a sixties type of commune. Others just thought we were strange. Questions began to surface. "Why would Ridge and Robanne sell their home just to move closer to their friends? Is this a little clique?"

Some of the church members thought our commitment to this type of community was great. It was the first time they had seen a model of Christian commitment fleshed out in a living situation. The eight of us enjoyed doing things together like collecting money for the refugee situation in Thailand and serving at church dinners.

Students were intrigued by the Community. They were curious about why we lived so differently from their parents. It was a great object lesson for the high school students to see us be Christlike to each other.

The Community was a great diversion from ministry. It helped prevent burnout in my life. Robanne and I have never experienced that intensity of fellowship or *koinonia* in our lives since then. In some ways the Community left a scar of desire to have that same *koinonia* in the other churches in which we've worked.

PASTORAL REVIEW

My whole life was going well at this time. I was becoming more cognizant of others as people, not just parts of a program. The Community was making me more accountable to a peer group. The elders were writing me affirming notes, and people in the congregation were pleased with my work. I wasn't without critics, but the critics seemed to be more tolerable.

Midway through the year, I met with Pastor Chuck Wickman for my annual pastoral review. Chuck always took each one of his staff members out to lunch and worked through a performance review

HEALTHY DIVERSIONS FROM MINISTRY

Diversions from ministry are necessary in order for a youth pastor to remain fresh and revitalized. The first step in developing healthy diversions from ministry is to assess your interests. Determine the things that are really in tune with your heart. If your interest is in the area of evangelism, maybe you can help sponsor a Billy Graham Association evangelistic crusade. Or perhaps you can be involved in an evangelistic outreach sponsored by a local church.

The second step in developing diversions is to ask your church leadership, "What would help me develop into a better person?" For some youth pastors, the answer is to go back to seminary for a master's or doctorate. For others it may be travel. Ask your leadership where you need to develop in your ministry.

The third step in developing diversions from ministry is to develop relationships with your family and friends. Robanne has always been significant in helping me understand where my diversions need to be. The Community helped me focus on people and situations outside of my ministry.

form. It was never very threatening to me because Chuck and I were buddies. I felt I knew my strong points and my weaknesses even before those sessions, but the reviews gave us good opportunities to reevaluate those areas.

For this particular review, we went to a local restaurant not too far from our church. As we nestled into a booth, I remember feeling really happy about the way God was directing my life. But Chuck had the ability to know that I needed something else in my life. He discerned that if I continued to simply maintain my ministry and programs without other interests in my life, I would stagnate.

Chuck and I went over the review papers and then he put them back in his briefcase. "Ridge," he said, "I want you to go to India with me." He felt that my worldview would be broadened if I joined him on this missionary journey around the world. Sponsored by a group called Responsive Christians, the trip would take me to Tokyo; Hong Kong; Thailand; India; and L'Abri, Switzerland. Chuck and I would be speaking for two or three days in each of the places we stopped with the exception of India, where we would spend one week in evangelistic meetings.

There was one drawback. In order to go, I would have to miss part of the Mexicali student mission trip. Mexicali, of course, was the jewel of my youth ministry at Walnut Creek. Students looked forward to it each year. It was highly visible to the church, and everybody was excited about what God was doing on these short-term mission projects. Yet they viewed Mexicali as "Ridge's program." How could it survive without me being there?

"Can't we do this another time when it won't conflict with Mexicali?" I responded to Chuck. I wasn't sure if I was willing to let go.

"Let's leave that decision to the elders," Chuck said. "We'll tell them our dream of making you a better pastor, and if they give us approval, we'll know it's God's will that we go on this trip together."

So we presented the plan to the elders knowing that I would have to miss one of the key events of Walnut Creek's youth ministry. I wanted to go with Chuck, but I wasn't sure how the elders would respond to our proposal. After the elders' meeting at which I wasn't present, Chuck slipped a note with the word *yes* under my office door. I was very, very excited that the board wanted me to go preach around the world.

This experience was significant because it caused me to learn how to delegate responsibility. I always thought the Mexicali trip required my presence, and had never dreamed of not being on the scene. But I quickly learned that the trip required only my staff. In fact, running their own mission trip gave the students a much greater sense of ownership.

Not only did they have ownership of the *Mexicali* trip, the students also had ownership of my journey around the world. Their vision was expanded by my not being with them. They met every day to pray for me while I was in Tokyo, Hong Kong, and other countries. They took turns writing me letters of encouragement. Each of the 28 days I was gone, I had an envelope to open, each one filled with two or three letters from a student encouraging me about my overseas ministry.

I did the same thing for my students, writing them letters for every day that I would be gone. Read in Sunday School, during training sessions, and at Mexicali, these letters fostered communication and prayer. I felt as if I was part of the student mission team even though we were going different directions.

BROKEN BY THE THIRD WORLD

In my fourth year at Walnut Creek what happened to my heart caught me off guard. I had no way of knowing I would never be the same after that year. I went on the world trip with very few expectations, thinking I would have a lot of fun and see some sights. Instead, it became the first of several experiences that caused my heart to ache.

My first stop was Tokyo. There I spent time with missionaries whom our church supported, and spoke at Tokyo Christian College. When I got off the airplane in Tokyo, brokenness first came in the form of aloneness; I felt more alone than I had ever felt before. Cut off by the language difference, I couldn't read any signs and was unable to communicate with anyone. It was the first time I'd ever been alone in a foreign country with the exception of Mexico and Canada. I felt lost—overwhelmed by the crowded conditions and highly mechanized society of the Orient.

My next stop was Hong Kong, where I met Chuck. During our visit, a missionary who worked in an area called the New Territories, offered to take us to see some of the boat people he worked with.

It was a boat ride I'll never forget—one that pushed my emotions to new levels. I'd never been exposed to anything like it before. Mexico had a lot of poverty and I had seen some tough sights, but not like what I was seeing in Hong Kong. The deteriorating boats, the smell, the overcrowded conditions, and the lack of what appeared to be concern for any kind of life were difficult for me to handle. The dirty water was the consistency of warm jello, filled with dead animals and raw sewage. Little kids swam through the filth to our boat and asked us for money. As I struggled to keep my feelings under control, I realized part of me desperately wanted out of there. At the same time, I was angry—asking, *God, why are You allowing people to live this way?* The situation at Michoacan de o' Campo was changeable. But riding in the junk around the harbor, I felt powerless to do anything. Later, I thought, *God, let's do something to change this.*

From Hong Kong we went to Thailand to visit the Saekeo refugee camp where I was impressed with the magnitude of world hunger. We saw over 50,000 displaced people in this camp run by the Red Cross and United Nations. Feeling like a tourist with my shorts and camera, I walked all afternoon down row after row of bamboo huts crammed with hungry people. Ironically, I had no idea that six or seven years later, I would be working in Wheaton

Bible Church's Sidewalk Sunday School with some of the same people from that camp.

As I tried to deal with everything I saw and experienced, I was drawn to Scripture focused on poor and oppressed people. I studied Jesus' examples of ministry to the sick, the oppressed, the jailed, the hungry, and the widows. Though I had never before seen political oppression or displaced families, I began to realize that most of the world lived not like I did in the United States, but like the people I had seen in Hong Kong and Thailand. It was these people living in refugee camps and suffering in overcrowded conditions who would probably be the object of Christ's affection today.

God was working in my heart. During the trip I reviewed Ronald Sider's *Rich Christians in an Age of Hunger* (InterVarsity Press), really thinking about the balance of power. I began considering how I might be able to make a difference in the world hunger problem and possibly mobilize students to minister to the poor and oppressed.

From Thailand we went to India. Each time the plane stopped, we went further and further back from civilization. We ended up in a little village called Chilakeluripet where we preached for a week. Though living conditions were poor, I saw thousands of people stand up to testify about Jesus Christ's work in their lives. We went to a baptismal service where the Christians marched through town, almost shouting to the non-Christians, "We believe in Jesus Christ."

One night while I was preaching, a snake slithered into the tent. Without stopping my sermon, making only a little commotion, some men killed it, threw it out, and went right back to being attentive. It took me by surprise that these people were so hungry for the Gospel that even a snake could not disturb their concentration. Up to this point, it was things I had observed that had broken me. Suddenly, I was confronted with preaching to hundreds of people each night, knowing that they were going to take every sermon that I preached and share it with hundreds of other people. I began to see that I could be part of the solution to the problem of hurting and oppressed people.

Next, we went to a leper colony. After we spoke, a man came up and wanted to read some Scripture to me, but he couldn't turn the pages of his Bible with his little stub of a hand. Then the people took an offering for our church back home. One lady gave an earring. I saw other jewelry and articles of clothing in the offering. They gave whatever they could. I couldn't believe these people wanted to give us money. I just wanted to give it back, but I realized this was their expression of thanks to the Walnut Creek Church members for allowing Chuck and me to visit them.

This was a great time for me as I grew closer to Chuck Wickman. Rooming together, we spent hours talking about what God was teaching us and how we could build a stronger relationship with each other.

Finally, we flew to L'Abri, Switzerland to spend a few days. Because Francis Schaeffer's family was having a reunion, I was able to talk over and process the things I had experienced in Japan, Hong Kong, Thailand, and India with some knowledgeable people. It helped to have time to sort out my thoughts and feelings.

The last leg of my journey was Mexico, to see my student teams faithfully working in Mexicali. After being away from my students for four weeks, I found the Mexicali mission project was running on schedule, and probably better than it would have with my direction. This was a real confirmation to me of God's working through delegation. I thought to myself, *I can be the vision maker without being the vision supervisor.*

I was amazed at how God was working in my life as I viewed the situations in Thailand, India, and the other countries. The whole principle of brokenness was new for me. Before, I had never cried over others unless they were hurt and I happened to love them. Suddenly, God was breaking my heart and causing me to feel a tenderness for these people in poverty with whom I didn't have a personal relationship.

BROKEN BY DELAYNE'S ILLNESS

The second experience that caused brokenness in my heart involved Delayne Roethe. One Friday afternoon, I received a phone call from Delayne. She was at a local Navy hospital and had just been diagnosed as having active diabetes. "Mom and Dad are with me," she said, "but I wish you would come out here."

Delayne wanted me there in addition to her parents because she knew her parents *had* to love her. The Roethes gave Delayne lots of love and support through this ordeal, but she needed someone besides family to care about her. In our relationship, I had shared with her my weaknesses and failures, so she knew I would love and accept her, even when she was sick.

There were no tears at first, but we were both scared. As we hugged and prayed together in the hall, we decided that we could make it through this ordeal together. Over the next few months,

Delayne changed from being a highly motivated, energy-filled person. Her eating habits had to be restricted, her exercise had to be monitored, and she lost much of her spontaneity because of the regimentation placed on her by the disease.

During the previous year, Delayne had supported me through some very rough times. I knew that God had used Delayne to help me with what I was going through. Now God was using me to help Delayne through her rough times. We spent time crying together and simply being with each other as I tried to encourage and support her. I had never committed myself to long-term relationships with students, but I suddenly found myself wanting to spend time with Delayne. I also realized that God sometimes creates brokenness in students as well as youth pastors.

WHEN IT'S TIME TO LEAVE

A youth pastor knows it's time to leave when God gives him a vision for a new or different ministry. Pastors who leave a church without a vision are probably not leaving with God's direction. It may be a new group of students, an expanded evangelistic program, or a missions program. He doesn't leave because he's restless. If that were the case, many youth pastors would leave every 30 days.

Secondly, God provides an opportunity to fulfill a vision. I don't think God will give a youth pastor a vision without a place to fulfill it. He may not provide that place immediately, but it's a pastor's responsibility to seek a specific place to go.

Thirdly, a youth pastor needs to have the necessary support to fulfill that vision. That support includes financial needs as well as the emotional support of family and mature brothers and sisters in Christ.

Finally, a youth pastor needs to have the right timing for his vision. There needs to be a sensitivity that this is a time when he can wrap things up and complete his current ministry. This can only be done by being open with the senior pastor and board. It is possible to have the vision, the support, the place, and the wrong timing. I've had many opportunities through the years to move to phenomenal churches and creative ministries. At the same time, I've learned to depend on the wise counsel of people in my life who helped me get a proper perspective on those offers.

A DECISION TO LEAVE

During this year I was struggling with making a decision to leave Walnut Creek. I made that decision in probably my finest year of ministry. I had critics and there were times when I was frustrated, but generally speaking, I was very encouraged and excited about the things God was doing in my life and ministry.

At the same time, I was concerned about our church building program. Though I was not highly involved in the planning, I was excited about the effects of physical growth on the ministries of the church. The staff vision was that the church would increase its membership to 2—3,000 in the next few years. The church was going to need a facility to accommodate that growth.

But, as usual, one person would criticize the program because there were no plans for a kitchen. Another person didn't like the color scheme or the landscape. I thought to myself, *Why can't these people understand that this is not just a building; it's part of the vision of the whole forward thinking of the church!*

I was very frustrated that we could not communicate that vision to the congregation. The elders were 100 percent behind the program, but perhaps we were just a bit ahead of the congregation. A meeting was called for the congregation to vote on the building program. The vote was taken and the program passed by only one vote. Obviously, this was not good enough for us to go ahead and build. From that point on, I began asking myself, "Can the kinds of ministries that I want to do be sustained in the present facility?" I soon knew that the vision that we as a staff had for the church was shrinking, and it was time for me to investigate leaving.

But I thought to myself, *How can I leave these kids? I've invested four years in some of them. How will the ministry be carried on? Who will take my place? Where will I go?* All these questions haunted me as I began to try to understand what God was doing.

Because God had increased my vision for the world in India and Thailand, Robanne and I began to feel a need to take a sabbatical to investigate what God might be doing in our lives. We felt it was important to demonstrate to our students that we were serious about our worldwide commitment—that the things we had learned in Mexicali could be fleshed out in our own lives. This sabbatical, we decided, would involve a foreign mission experience that would last three to six months, perhaps even a year. Robanne and I had now been married six years. We had been immersed in ministry ever since we had been married, either in preparing for or doing ministry. But we had never taken the time to look into whether or not we wanted to start a family. Most people perceived us as a childless couple for life, and we had sort of decided to remain childless in order to facilitate more ministry. However, that decision

REMAINING SINGLE OR CHILDLESS IN MINISTRY

Robanne and I struggled for over five years with the family issue. As we considered the possibility of not having children, we found the following advantages for a youth pastor to remain single or childless.

1. Your time is very flexible. You can meet students at any hour, day or night, without interference in the family schedule.

2. You can become a "safe other." Students tend not to link you with their parents, so you can enjoy contact with them as peers.

3. Your home is more accessible to students. Kids can stop in without barging in on a family.

Robanne and I experienced enough disadvantages in not having children that we constantly reconsidered our approach to starting a family. We found some of the following disadvantages for a youth pastor to remain single or childless:

1. People tend to think that you are perpetually younger than you really are.

2. Some people pressure their pastoral staffs to start families so they can better relate to the family interests and problems.

3. Your relationships with students' parents are limited because you haven't experienced parenthood.

4. You tend to neglect your own needs to develop family relationships.

was made within the confines of working in ministry, and our environment dictated our choices. Now we thought it was a good time for us to come to grips with whether or not God wanted us to have a family.

Slowly, we began to explore the possibility of going overseas. We made a couple of phone calls to some mission boards, and one day I got a call from Nairobi, Kenya. An African voice asked me whether Robanne and I would be willing to come and teach at Scott

Theological College, a school run by the Africa Inland Mission in Machakos, Kenya. I was excited to think about the possibilities of going to Africa, but in order for us to make the trip, we would have to make all our preparations, including raising our money and selling our house, within approximately six weeks.

Robanne and I prayed about it and sought the counsel of our pastors, parents, and several key people in our church. The Community helped us pray through our decision, and we submitted ourselves to their authority. They affirmed our call to a sabbatical. So on July 24, we submitted our resignation to the elders of the Walnut Creek church.

As we submitted our resignation letter, I was reminded of how Nehemiah went to rebuild the walls in Jerusalem. Even though he was cupbearer to the king in an influential city, he had compassion on his homeland. However, he did not get up and leave his influential position just because Jerusalem was his first passion. He spent time with the king, bringing him into the decision-making process. Because he took time to share his goals, the king supported Nehemiah's venture, not only emotionally, but physically with men, supplies, and protection.

In the same way, Robanne and I tried to share our goals and reasons for leaving Walnut Creek in the letter. The congregation supported our decision, and the Sunday before we left they gave us a check for almost $9,000. This completely paid for our entire trip. What a thrill to see the way God had worked and moved in our lives!

SAYING GOOD-BYE
How do you say good-bye after four years? The church held a farewell dinner for us. The staff and students had decorated the tables with classy silverware and nice dishes, but in true incongruous style, the meal consisted of pizza and soft drinks. There was lots of fun and laughter, and after the meal, a number of students testified as to the effectiveness of our ministry. One of the adult staff members put together an excellent multimedia presentation of all the important faces and meaningful events that had taken place in our lives over the past four years.

On the screen, I saw face after face that had been changed because of what God had done through our ministry. God had given us some great adult staff members, but I was particularly excited to see the student leadership and their obvious expressions of love and gratitude. I wanted to say thanks to the students and their families for allowing us the privilege of working with such fine students. I had put my thoughts in a letter, but when the time came to read it, I was so choked up that I couldn't express myself. I just began to cry, and one of the elders had to finish reading my letter to the church.

Until this point, I had never quite comprehended how much of my heart I had given to the students. Beyond the pain of criticism, I had received tremendous joy from my ministry. It was fantastic to learn that the basis for youth ministry is a love for students, not because it's my job, but because I wanted to love kids.

DEVELOPING A TENDER HEART

During this year I discovered that I need distractions from youth ministry to give me a sense of awareness and brokenness in my life. I learned that one way to develop a tender heart is to put myself in touch with broken people. In Psalm 34:18, the psalmist tells us that "the Lord is close to the brokenhearted." When I feel distant from God, it's usually because I have put distance between God's broken people and myself.

During my last year at Walnut Creek, Mexicali became more than just a youth program. God used *me*, not a student, to minister in the life of Anna, the little girl mentioned in my journal. Eventually, the mission program became an expression of my own heart—my own way of alleviating some of the needs of the Third World.

I came back from my world trip with a real burden for the Third World. My heart had many aches. I had seen people whose only tools for ministry were the Bible, a Coleman lantern, and a bicycle. And God blessed them just as much or more than our Walnut Creek Church with all its resources. There was brokenness in my heart that I had never felt before. The brokenness that I felt in India affected my ministry so that I began to run mission programs for high school students on an advanced level where their hearts could be broken.

I needed the experience of retreating to the Third World to rekindle my spirit. Other youth pastors may simply need to put themselves in local situations where broken people are present. My relationships with Anna and Delayne brought brokenness into my life, but they also gave me opportunities to support and encourage broken kids. Ministering to broken people and students can encourage a youth pastor and allow him to broaden his perspective on his ministry. As a result, he will begin to search more deeply and more diligently to allow God to work in his life.

A second way in which I developed brokenness is through understanding that I'm a model for students in everything I do. In Matthew 10:5-8, Jesus sent out His disciples to preach, heal the sick, raise the dead, cleanse lepers, and cast out demons. But before they departed on their journey, Jesus spent time training the disciples and demonstrating His compassion. In the same way, a youth pastor must model godly character and principles to his students. For example, during my four years at Walnut Creek, I had taken six missionary trips with students. As a result, students' hearts were broken for the mission field, and several were considering full-time Christian service. To encourage those who were considering missionary careers and short-term overseas assignments, Robanne and I felt we needed to demonstrate our commitment to the Third World through a sabbatical.

I also learned to develop brokenness by putting myself in vulnerable situations. In the Book of Hosea, we read the story of how the prophet was ordered to marry an adulterous wife. Though Gomer proved unfaithful, the broken prophet was instructed to love his wife and bring her into reconciliation. When Hosea made himself vulnerable, the Lord used the prophet's marital relationship to express His compassion and love for the unfaithful nation of Israel.

During this year of ministry, I found myself becoming more vulnerable as Robanne and I committed ourselves to the Community. When you live with a group of people, it is difficult to hide your weaknesses from them. Suddenly, all my failures were visible not just to Robanne, but to the other three couples. The eight of us had determined to be who God wanted us to be as a *group*—not as *individuals*. We were responsible for the spiritual welfare of each couple and shared in each other's hurts. As I became more honest in my relationships and confided in the Community, my heart was burdened with a desire to be broken and to serve broken people.

SMALL CHURCH SPOTLIGHT

RIDGE: Pam, do you have a job review annually?

PAM: I haven't had a review in two years. But that doesn't stop church members from telling me how I'm doing in my job.

RIDGE: I think every youth worker, whether professional, volunteer, or part-time, ought to have a time when the people to whom he is accountable review him.

PAM: I agree! I need the opportunity to make my concerns known to the people who make decisions about youth ministry.

RIDGE: Maybe you should ask for a review by your pastor, Christian education committee, or elders or deacons, whoever is responsible for your youth program. It will help you tell the church where you're at, and they can tell you whether you are doing a good job or not.

PAM: Then maybe I'll experience more brokenness! **How do you see the principle of brokenness applying to a volunteer or part-time person?**

RIDGE: The principle of brokenness applies to ministry whether you can give 10 hours a week or 50 hours a week. God wants to minister through a person whose heart is tender, rather than the person who thinks he is going to change the world through programming.

PAM: One of my problems in a small church is the tendency to be program-oriented. I sometimes think that if the kids have enough stuff to do, they will be changed. I don't know how to create opportunities for brokenness for myself or my students.

RIDGE: All the things that broke me were not programs, but people. So you can't travel around the world or take your youth group to India or Thailand. Have you ever thought about bringing broken people to your youth group? Maybe a refugee. I know several families who swam for two days to get out of Vietnam. They were finally picked up by a boat. You could ask the kids in those families to talk to your youth group. Through their vivid storytelling, your kids can relive the experience of being there.

There are all kinds of good mission organizations that can provide small groups with ministry opportunities in inner-city areas, rural America, or overseas. There's no reason that a youth group of five or six people can't take a trip to Appalachia or to inner-city Chicago and be broken together.

To experience personal brokenness and vulnerability, a youth worker in a small church can work to develop relationships with a small group as Robanne and I did in the Community.

Do you think a part-time person experiences the same lack of relationship-building that a full-time youth pastor experiences?

PAM: In this chapter you seem to indicate that you often feel individual loneliness because you're away from your own peer group. You have this great staff and you're ministering daily to students, but you're still lonely.

There's a different kind of loneliness that occurs in a small church. Because the fellowship is more intimate, I know everybody in the church and they know me. But I still experience corporate loneliness. Sometimes I feel as if I'm the only one who cares for my students.

RIDGE: In that case, do you find it necessary to have diversions from youth ministry?

PAM: I don't think diversions from youth ministry are as important for the person in the small church, particularly if you're part-time like I am. Your problem as a full-time pastor is that you "live" high school kids all day, and sometimes you just need to get away from students and explore some other creative outlets.

I already have the diversion of a full-time job. Usually, it's the stress of trying to balance a full-time job, a part-time youth ministry, and freelance writing that creates in me a need to escape. I don't need any more diversions in my life.

RIDGE: In fact, you may need to eliminate some outside interests in order to be effective.

CREATE IN ME
RENEWAL

TUESDAY, August 30
Robanne and I had our first dinner in Kenya with Dick and Ellen Norton. Earlier this afternoon, we picked up the Nortons' dog, Pal. I am surprised that most of the missionaries seem to have dogs or cats. I'm even more amazed at Dick and Ellen's emphasis on their family life. Even though the missionaries' children are in boarding school, most families seem to spend more time together than my students' families in the United States.

I'm thankful that Dick and Ellen have been so helpful in getting us settled. If they weren't here, we would really feel lonely. Maybe that's normal. After all, we're tired, we don't really know anyone, the situation is totally strange, we aren't in the house in which we expected to live, our schedule is completely different, and we don't really know what is going on.

I feel as if I've lost control of my circumstances and the mobility to escape my situation. For the next three months, we're stuck here for better or worse. I wonder how we will feel at the end of this adventure. Will we be relieved to go home? Or will we lose our heart to Kenya as many of the missionaries have?

THE PROBLEM WITH YOUTH MINISTRY is the job is too big for one person to handle. That's one reason youth pastors suffer burnout. There's a mundaneness about working with kids. By the time a youth pastor spends the afternoon listening to three kids in his group describe their problems with their little sisters, he gets a little bored.

A sabbatical or periodic renewal can change a youth pastor's life by giving him a distraction from the routine and redundancy of youth ministry. Our short-term missionary sabbatical provided us with a renewal experience as well as a distraction from ministry. Kenya was a tremendous risk. Not too many people sell their house, put their furniture in storage, and take off to Africa for three months! It smacks against the status quo.

But some of the greatest memories Robanne and I have made during our married lives are of our sabbatical. Swimming at a beach in Africa. Castle-hopping in Scandinavia. Taking a safari into the bush. In this chapter I want to share how I learned to make memories with my family, with my ministry, with myself, and with God. Making memories not only brings about diversions from ministry, but it makes provision for future renewal. I can be renewed by just thinking about Kenya.

PREPARING FOR RENEWAL

On August 25, Robanne and I arrived in New York City to begin our African adventure. We prepared for our sabbatical with the understanding that we could stay in Africa for a year if we wanted to. The minimum time we had to spend in Africa was three months. At a brief orientation meeting at the Africa Inland Mission headquarters, we met 15 missionaries who were returning to the field. When it came time to make our travel and financial arrangements, we were pleased to present a check for the full amount of

TIME TO TAKE A SABBATICAL?

Periodical sabbaticals are necessary for a youth pastor in order for him to be able to continue to meet the demands of full-time ministry. Here are 10 indications that it may be time to take a sabbatical:

1. Meddling in other people's affairs.
2. Lacking your own spiritual devotions or spending less time in prayer and God's Word.
3. Defensiveness with coworkers.
4. Avoiding students or breaking appointments.
5. Marital conflicts.
6. More emotional than usual.
7. Finding yourself with confirmed satanic attacks.
8. Increased counseling load.
9. Lack of organization or office messier than usual.
10. Bragging about ministry to contemporaries.

our needed support.

On August 27, we boarded a plane for Amsterdam where we caught a flight to Kenya. As the sun came up on August 29, many of the missionaries recognized with excitement landmarks and familiar sights. After landing in Nairobi and proceeding through immigration, baggage, and customs, the returning missionaries were met by a large group of family and friends. We felt a little lonesome; even the *new* missionaries seemed to have family and friends waiting. For the past two days all the missionaries had become sort of a family, but when we arrived in Nairobi, the warmth and close fellowship that we had experienced was disseminated because of existing relationships.

As we drove through Nairobi, we saw a fairly modern city on a plain with a few mountains in the background. The missionaries as well as the nationals were in Western dress. *Where are the grass huts and naked women?* I wondered. I felt foreign but also felt accepted because I was part of the missionary group.

From Nairobi, we drove 25 miles to the village where we would be living. During this short drive, we were amazed to see all the wildlife, including an ostrich and a giraffe that crossed the highway. We arrived in Machakos and moved into a little bungalow at the edge of the mission station which houses Scott Theological College. We were disappointed that the house where we were to live had already been taken by missionaries who had arrived two weeks earlier. As a result, we had to borrow linens and a stove. That night, as we wearily dropped into bed, I asked the Lord to help Robanne and me live out what He had intended us to do in Africa.

A RENEWED MINISTRY

My job at Scott Theological College was to teach ethics and English Bible classes, while Robanne worked in the library and taught typing. We also spoke in many churches and helped with the seminary's Christian education department as much as we could. On an average day I taught in the morning, studied in the afternoon, and spent time socially with the other missionaries in the evening.

While we were in Africa, I developed my skills in preaching and teaching. I found myself teaching college students and spending a lot of time preaching through an interpreter. I studied a lot and knew the content, but I felt unequipped because I was in unfamiliar territory. Suddenly, the students were black and had British accents. Their homes were huts. They talked about how a gazelle once ran through their classroom.

One of my goals for ministry in Africa was to meet a special African brother whom I could pray for on a regular basis when I returned to the United States. Lawrence Bomett, one of our interpreters, became that brother. We had some fun experiences with Lawrence, and I appreciated the opportunity to minister to him.

While on the mission field I was able to chart my own course and maintain my own creative style. I broke the seminary students into small groups and they responded well to the learning process. As I spent time at the dorms talking to students, I sensed God was affirming my gifts of creativity and innovation. I felt fortunate to discover affirmation of my skills outside the context of youth ministry.

Though I was glad to get a rest from programs and the time commitment of youth ministry, I found myself missing the students. One day we took a soccer team up from Machakos to Rift Valley Academy, the Christian high school for missionary kids in Kijabe. While the guys were warming up I took a walk around the school. I went into one of the dorms and just sat and listened to the kids talk about American rock music. It brought back memories of Delayne Roethe and rekindled my whole love for high school students. I realized kids are kids wherever they are.

I also became more aware of how my lifestyle was being closely observed by students. Western missions had affected the Kenyans in regard to clothes, behavior, and vocabulary. I was particularly embarrassed that Kenyans had integrated our religious talk into their vocabulary. Spiritual cliches, like "praise the Lord" and "Lord willing," had become part of the African culture.

I wondered what kind of bad spiritual habits the students at Walnut Creek were involved in because of my ministry. At the same time, I hoped that the students had picked up some positive habits from me like Bible study and dreaming big ideas for God.

Our biggest adjustments to Africa were not in the areas of clothes, food, or climate. The major changes we experienced were in our schedules and pace of ministry. While the mission field in general was very exciting and educational, the pace of life was so slow that it drove Robanne and me crazy. We went to bed when the sun went down and got up when the sun came up. We soon discovered an easy way to go into Nairobi and took advantage of that trip at least once a week. In the city we spent time just walking around reading newspapers, watching people, and trying to do as

HENRY, WASN'T IT NICE OF THE YOUTH GROUP TO SEND
US ON THIS ROMANTIC WEEKEND?

many different things as possible. One of the veteran missionaries
said that Robanne and I saw more and traveled more in our three
months in Kenya than he had in his last two four-year terms. So we
felt that we had made good use of our time.

While a slower pace was what Robanne and I needed for a
sabbatical, it was not how we wanted to spend our lives. If we had
ever entertained any notions about becoming career missionaries,
we quickly rethought them. It was a long three months, and yet, as
I look back on that time, it was an invaluable learning experience.

During our sabbatical, Robanne and I continually sought God's
direction for our lives. After much prayer, we wrote to Wheaton
Bible Church in Wheaton, Illinois, and told them that we would
like to candidate. At first, I had been turned off by Wheaton Bible
Church. They had called me during the previous year and said that
they were looking for a youth pastor. "The present youth pastor is
irreplaceable," a church representative told me. "He's one of a
kind, and we don't know how we will replace him." They wanted
someone who would come in and build on the foundation already
laid.

I told them I wasn't interested. The church needed to put some
time and space between that "one-of-a-kind" person and the next

youth pastor. Little did I know that 18 months later they would call me again. It had taken a year and a half for God to bring me to the point where I was ready to accept that challenge.

Wheaton Bible Church was so anxious to hear from us that they called and asked if we would candidate when we left Africa. We knew then that we'd at least have a place to go and visit when we returned to the United States.

On the way home from Africa, we decided to take one week to go on safari and spend some time out in the bush. What an incredible memory I have of spending a week all alone with my wife looking at God's creation of wildlife in Africa. It's a memory that Robanne and I will never forget.

After leaving Kenya we went to Scandinavia where we spent 10 days visiting Denmark, Sweden, and Norway. While we were anxious to get home and settled into a new position, we were also very concerned that we make more memories as a couple. When we arrived in the United States, we spent two days in New York and then went to Detroit to visit my family. After a few days we went to the Chicago area to candidate at the Wheaton Bible Church.

A RENEWED MARRIAGE
During our time in Africa, Robanne and I fell in love with each other in a deeper way. I knew down deep in my heart that I needed to invest more time with Robanne. At Walnut Creek, I had given her the time I had left over after programs, Bible studies, basketball games, golf, and mission trips. In Kenya, we had no car, phone, TV, or radio—just each other.

Our three months in Africa were extremely meaningful for our marriage. We spent hours catching up on four years of uncommunicated areas, talking about the same subjects, coming to different conclusions after each discussion. We thought about how we wanted to minister and grow together and what we wanted our marriage to be. We learned to have fun together, laughing and enjoying each other's company.

For Robanne, going to Africa was a small risk compared to being married to me. When we first got married, being a youth pastor's wife was a risk, though she still had the comforts of home and family. Being in Africa all by herself, getting only written support from her family and friends, was also a risk—but one that showed her that risk-taking can be worthwhile.

Robanne also experienced some of the brokenness for the Third

World that I had felt during my trip to India, Hong Kong, and Thailand. One weekend one of my students, Ronald, invited me to preach at his church and visit his home. The three of us shared one motorcycle to his village. Ronald's family had two huts—a cooking hut and a sleeping hut. Robanne decided to take a look at the cooking hut since Ronald's family had killed their goat for our dinner. The inside of the hut was like the inside of a chimney. Grease was hanging down from the roof, chickens were running around, and it was really dirty. Since the prize part of the goat is the fat, our hosts gave us, their honored guests, slabs of goat fat for our dinner. On the way home, Robanne said, "Most of the world lives like Ronald's family. We don't know how fortunate we really are."

WAYS TO STRENGTHEN YOUR MARRIAGE/FAMILY LIFE

Robanne and I have found it very important to work together to build and renew our marriage. As you work in youth ministry, build some of the following activities into your schedule.

1. Take time to talk with your spouse and family. Fill them in on the intimate details of what is going on in your life and ministry.

2. Put your family on the church and high school student mailing list so they can help you with scheduling conflicts.

3. Schedule a sabbatical weekend each year during which you and your spouse or family go some place by yourselves.

4. Schedule a three-month sabbatical every four years of ministry.

5. Set aside an evening each week for you and your family to ask the question, "How are we getting along?" This time of sharing gives each person the opportunity to express affirmation or displeasure.

6. Do something outside your ministry realm that is fun to do as a couple or family, like jogging, biking, playing golf, or playing tennis.

7. Travel together. If you speak at conferences or attend conventions, invite your spouse or family along. The fellowship will be great.

One of the major reasons that we went to Africa was to talk about having a family. Robanne and I had been married seven years. By our own choice, we had become so isolated in youth ministry that we hadn't taken time to investigate whether or not we should start a family. We knew that children would drastically alter our ministry. Kenya provided us not only with an opportunity to live out our faith in the context of the Third World, but it gave us time to pray and discuss whether God wanted us to have a family.

Robanne and I felt strongly that we did not want to have children. But we wondered if we were being selfish in wanting to protect our mobility, or if we really wanted to devote more time to our ministry. We worked so well as a team. Would a child destroy that team? Would it limit our mobility together? Would it mean that I would be the youth pastor and Robanne would have to stay home?

We began to rethink our roles. Robanne and I have always shared our chores around the house. Since Robanne is more skilled in math and organizing the household, she handles all the shopping, finances, and legal matters of our home. Since I'm more interested in the decorating and the way our home looks, my chores include vacuuming, washing dishes, cleaning the cars, and outdoor maintenance. We've never been hung up on traditional roles, but when it came to children, would we have to move to more traditional roles? Would we have to leave youth ministry in order to have children?

Robanne had a lot of maternal instincts, and all her life, she had been told that part of being a fulfilled woman was to have children. If she didn't have children, what would fulfill that instinctive need in her? We talked about Robanne's need for distractions and diversions in her life. What kind of career would she like to have? Did she want to continue being involved in youth ministry? Should we be co-youth pastors? Should Robanne form a women's ministry? Our decision not to have children forced us to consider many alternatives.

After much prayer and a lot of discussion, we decided that God didn't want us to try to have children at this time. We were both 29 years old and felt that we had until age 35 to have a family. We determined to keep children a matter of prayer and then when we were 34 years old, we would try for one year to have children. If God gave us a child during that year, we would be very grateful. If He didn't we would receive that as a sign that God wanted us to remain childless in order to devote our time to the ministry in a more creative way.

God also enriched the spiritual areas of our marriage. Robanne and I had never been real big on having devotions or prayer together. Maybe we had gotten into a bad habit in our first years of ministry by assuming that we were both spiritual and, therefore, because we were spiritual individuals we had a spiritual marriage. I had fallen into the trap that I didn't need to lead Robanne in her walk with God; I simply assumed that she was growing. We ran our spiritual lives independently, but we weren't afraid to come together to bring big decisions to God.

In Africa we found ourselves spending time together daily with God. One of the things that we had to do on the mission field was give our testimony at each church and home that we visited. The Africans were very concerned about how we came to know Jesus Christ as our personal Saviour. Therefore, Robanne and I were forced to talk about our spiritual lives in front of each other. These spiritual observations spilled over to our private conversations. We talked about the structure of the church. We prayed together about whether we would be able to relate to a large church like Wheaton Bible Church. Our spiritual growth began to evidence itself even on the mission field. Many times as we were introduced in chapel services, we could tell that our enthusiasm and individuality had made an impression on the other missionaries.

A NEW MINISTRY

When I arrived in Wheaton, I don't think I was prepared for being thrust into youth ministry quite so soon. It was difficult to shift from giraffes and gazelles to profiles of discipled students and Christian education committees.

Prior to our trip to Africa, I had filled out a lengthy questionnaire that was analyzed by a team of management experts to see what my abilities were in the area of youth ministry. One of the first things I did when candidating was to go over the results of that test. It showed that I was extremely creative and highly motivated by internalized goals and convictions. The team of experts felt that I would be able to handle the position that the church had open.

I was intimidated by the size of Wheaton Bible Church. To go from 1,000 members at Walnut Creek, California to a church of 2,000 in Wheaton, Illinois seemed overwhelming to me. Robanne and I wondered whether the principles we had practiced at Walnut Creek would apply to a larger church.

The executive pastor was officious and businesslike in his inter-

QUESTIONS TO ASK WHEN CANDIDATING

General questions about the church:

1. What is the general church program and organization?
2. What are the statistics of church membership and attendance?
3. Does the church have a constitution? (Obtain a copy.)
4. How is the Sunday School organized?
5. What's the church's policy regarding divorce and remarriage?
6. What is the church's doctrinal statement?
7. Does the church have a budget?
8. What is the financial condition of the church?
9. Are there plans for building in the near future?

Specific questions about the youth pastor position:

1. Is there a job description?
2. How long has the church been without a youth pastor?
3. How long was the previous youth pastor here?
4. Why did the previous youth pastor leave?
5. How many men have been considered for this youth pastorate since the former pastor left?
6. What is the attitude of the high school students toward the church at this time?
7. If a call to the church is accepted, will it be for an indefinite period of time?
8. Is a parsonage provided for the youth pastor?
9. Does the church make any provision for secretarial help?
10. Does the church give an annual vacation?
11. What is the church's policy on sabbaticals?
12. Is the youth group in the budget? What items are included?
13. Is the youth group expected to raise money? How?
14. How many and what kinds of meetings is the youth pastor expected to attend?
15. Are there any programs which the youth pastor is required to run?
16. What responsibilities and expectations does the church have for the youth pastor's wife and family?

viewing. It appeared that he was the one who ran the church. He ran the staff meetings and told me what my responsibilities would be. The senior pastor, Chris Lyons, didn't even meet me until the very last part of our weekend.

The church was within about nine months of starting construction on a needed building, so the offices for the ministry departments were in one house and the business offices were located in another house a block away. As Robanne and I walked over to the executive pastor's office for our last interview of the weekend, we stopped at the corner and agreed that we were coming to this church . . . that God was calling us to Wheaton. At the same time, I thought, *Will I ever be friends with the senior pastor . . . or be able to build the kind of relationships with the Wheaton staff that I had with the Walnut Creek staff?*

EXPERIENCING RENEWAL

I was renewed in several ways this year as a result of my sabbatical. In Africa I learned the importance of scheduling some major time away from ministry in order to be mentally, physically, and spiritually replenished. Just as the Hebrew law provided for the liberation of soil, slaves, and debtors every seven years (Exodus 23:10-11; Deuteronomy 15:12-18), churches need to provide a sabbatical year for youth pastors on a regular basis.

Many youth pastors are able to take a weekly day off or they can regiment their time so that they can leave most of their work at the office. I, on the other hand, am a workaholic; I'm usually at the church seven days a week, at least five nights a week. I spend hours on the phone and with students. For me to try to schedule one day off a week is next to impossible. But the main lesson I learned on the mission field is to slow down and pace myself in such a way that God can "renew [my] strength" (Isaiah 40:31).

One way I pace myself is by taking 15 minutes every day for "Think Time." I go in my office, turn off the light, and lock the door. Next I put the phone on transfer and lie down on the floor. Then I just ask myself the following questions: "What kind of ministry am I doing?" "Can I do my ministry better?" or, "Should I be doing this kind of ministry at all?"

The second area in which I was renewed was in my concept of God's faithfulness, provision, and worthiness of worship and praise. God faithfully provided for all our needs "according to His glorious riches in Christ Jesus" (Philippians 4:19). He performed a financial miracle for us so that we were able to pay every bill even though we had no salary. God sustained us in that step and we learned the principle of dependence.

As we became more familiar with African church services, our concept of worship was renewed. We were impressed with the centrality of God's Word and the importance of participation in the African worship services which sometimes lasted for several hours.

I went to Kenya with an open heart and mind to see what God was doing in my life. As I became more dependent on the Lord, I was drawn to the Wheaton Bible Church position. It seemed to be a job so big that only God could make me successful in it. I would need to show my dependence on Him. Eventually, Robanne and I felt that we could accept the challenge at Wheaton Bible Church because of the renewed confidence in God we had gained through our African experience.

Finally, our time in Africa gave Robanne and me a renewed outlook on our marriage and ministry. The sabbatical served as a way for me to understand how much I need Robanne and what a great gift of God she is.

Africa also made me want to celebrate life. I don't want to fall into the normal mechanical lifestyle that some youth pastors live, mundanely doing the same retreats each year, going to the same places, and teaching the same Bible lessons each Sunday morning. I want to have different kinds of experiences penetrating my life so I can stay on the cutting edge of youth ministry. Living in a community with three other couples, being involved with the senior pastor in a discipling relationship, broadening my world concern through short-term missions—all these experiences have brought renewal to my life and contributed to a uniqueness in my ministry.

SMALL CHURCH SPOTLIGHT

PAM: OK, Ridge, not too many part-time people can take off three months and go to Kenya so they can be renewed. **How can a volunteer find renewal in his life and ministry?**

RIDGE: If I were a part-time person, I would first make sure that I had a clear-cut termination of my commitment to the youth program.

PAM: Yeah, small churches refuse to look for someone to replace you until you're gone.

RIDGE: So tell them that you'll make a two-year commitment. And then at 18 months, tell them that again so that they're looking for recruits. Then take six months or a year off to be refreshed.

There are some other ways to build renewal in your ministry. Go to conventions. Go off on your own mission trip for a day. Go to a survival camp. Take your vacation and work in a camp as a speaker or maintenance man. Take a personal day once a month and retreat. In my case, I go to downtown Chicago or to the library and think and read about things that are important to me.

PAM: Maybe another way I could get a renewed outlook is by reading about other people's experiences. Even though I might not be able to touch the world physically, I can touch it through books.

RIDGE: Read biographies of great missionaries. Or spend time looking at *National Geographic*—not for the photographs, but for what it says about the various countries.

seven
CREATE IN ME
FLEXIBILITY

FRIDAY, *November 12*

Tonight the Wheaton Bible Church students gave Robanne and me a "Welcome Aboard" party. It was at a large house and there were about 80 students there. A few group members put this party together by calling every student on the mailing list and inviting them to come and meet their new youth pastor. Robanne and I had a fun evening mingling with the students and getting to know a few.

There was some good food and a few skits. The last skit of the evening was done by a high school senior. The student sat up in front of the group with a legal pad of paper. "I'd like to tell you the story of our youth group," he said. We sat and listened.

"This is Gus Espinosa, our youth pastor for a year," he said as he drew a stick figure on the legal pad. "He decided he liked under-privileged kids in Philadelphia better than us, so he went to work with them." The senior ripped off the page. Then he drew another stick figure. "This is Jim Glynn. He was our youth pastor for a year also. He was a good teacher, but he wanted to study more than he liked us, so he's gone now." He ripped off that page. Then he drew three stick figures on the next page. "This is Mark, Dale, and Patrick. They've been filling in for a year, but they don't like us anymore, so they're going their separate ways." He ripped off that page. Then he drew a long, skinny stick figure and said, "This is Ridge Burns. He's come to us from California. I wonder how long he'll stay."

The room got really quiet. I didn't know how to react. Obviously, the senior was a little intimidated by my presence at Wheaton Bible Church, and he was putting me to the test.

I'm so glad God gave me a good response. As the students watched to see my reaction, with confidence I said, "I'll stay as long as we can do what God intends for us to do."

Obviously, these students are carrying around some heavy baggage regarding the position of youth pastor. The senior class in particular has been raked over so many different styles of youth ministry that it's going to be difficult for me to gain a foothold. I hope the Lord will help me to be flexible enough to be their youth pastor.

INFLEXIBILITY USUALLY SHOWS UP in youth pastors whose ministries are more program-centered than need-centered. One of the things that helps me remain flexible is the realization that the kids I work with are constantly changing. At one point, they all dressed like Madonna and Michael Jackson. Six months later they went through their Bruce Springsteen stage. Now they're into someone else.

How I minister is in some ways related to how flexible I become. When you have had experience in a youth ministry, there is a tendency to try to duplicate what has taken place in the past. But that's erroneous since all kids are not the same. In Walnut Creek, some of the kids to whom I ministered were "salt" on their campuses. I could have just run the same program in Wheaton that I had run in Walnut Creek, but my ministry manifested itself in a

SURE I'LL BE HAPPY
TO KICK OFF THIS
YEAR'S SHOW!

totally different way. Because Wheaton is a strong Christian community, I had to take students on mission trips outside of the community to learn how to be servants of God.

As I became more flexible in my ministry, I saw my flexibility reflected in my students. When I arrived in Wheaton, some of the students had given up on the church or had negative stereotypes of the youth pastor. But when they saw that I was flexible enough to try to minister to them where they were, they responded to my efforts.

In this chapter, I want to share how flexibility made a difference in the way I approached my ministry at Wheaton Bible Church. I experienced many changes in my life this year—a new home in the Midwest, a new staff, new students, new parents, new programs. If I hadn't found ways to build flexibility into my life and ministry, I probably wouldn't have been nearly as successful.

UPROOTING

After our sabbatical in Africa, we returned to California to pick up our belongings. It was really hard to walk into the Walnut Creek Church after being gone for three months. Ken Stuckey, one of my interns, had become the interim youth pastor for a year. He was doing an excellent job running the youth programs, yet his ministry was very different from the way I had ministered at Walnut Creek. For example, I had put out a weekly newspaper that had professional artwork and typeset copy. Ken was now copying the newsletter on the office Xerox machine. It was the same information, just packaged differently. I'm not sure either method was any more effective than the other one.

The biggest change I saw was in my former office. The room in which I had spent so much time had taken on the image of Ken Stuckey with cowboy pictures on the wall. A few books stood on the once-crowded bookshelves, and the desk, which I had kept uncluttered, was now piled with paper.

None of this reflects negatively on Ken, because he had merely changed the office's image so it looked more comfortable to him. It was just hard for me, because my memories focused on what the office felt like when I was there, and I wanted to feel a little indispensible. I knew I didn't want to stay in Walnut Creek, that I needed a change, but I wanted Walnut Creek to stay the same.

As I drove my little blue pickup truck out of Walnut Creek for the last time, I struggled with mixed emotions. My thoughts went back to the church spaghetti dinner sponsored by my staff and students during my first year at Walnut Creek. As I remembered the appreciation and confidence for my ministry that were expressed to me at that time, I asked myself, *Will I ever have this type of experience or feel this kind of dedication to a church again?*

I thought of my relationships with the Linmans, Delayne Roethe, and Chuck Wickman, and how I really loved my students at Walnut Creek. *Will God ever give me a new group of students and friends like the ones that have been so important to me in Walnut Creek? Will I ever find another Delayne Roethe?*

Suddenly, I realized that Walnut Creek had captured my whole heart. I remembered Chuck Wickman saying, "The church will take as much of you as you let it." I felt incredibly alone as I drove away, filled with feelings of doubt and inadequacy. For the first time in my life, I was moving not because I had to, but because I felt God was leading me. While I felt a tremendous sense of direction from God, my heart ached at leaving my Walnut Creek ministry, and I wondered if I would be able to pour my heart into the ministry at Wheaton Bible Church.

CONFIRMATION OF A NEW CALLING

Robanne and I left the West Coast and started to drive east. By the time we crossed the Mississippi River, we began to feel God's confirmation of our decision to come to Wheaton Bible Church. I called our realtor in California, and she told me that she had received an offer on our condominium that she felt we ought to accept, and that we could close within two weeks. When I told Robanne about the offer, she just said, "Thank You, Lord!" We both felt very strongly it was just another confirmation from God.

We arrived in Wheaton the day of the annual church meeting. We checked into a hotel at 5:00 P.M., took showers, and rushed to the 6:00 P.M. meeting. It was held in a huge rented hall at the county complex. At Walnut Creek, our church meetings were held on Sunday nights with about 10 percent of the church members present. In contrast, there were probably 500 people at Wheaton Bible Church's dinner which included a multimedia show and entertainment by a magician. Later, I discovered that the executive pastor set the task of making the meeting a celebration as one of his main priorities.

When we arrived at the dinner, many church members welcomed us and told us how grateful they were that we had come. They called me up on the platform to give a word of greeting to the church. I don't remember what I said, but I felt as if I could have cried at any moment, and that was the last thing I wanted to do. First of all, I was very scared, and secondly, I just wasn't prepared for so much change in my life. I also sensed God working through the congregation to give me confirmation of His calling me to Wheaton Bible Church.

The church had gone through seven youth pastors in 10 years. Their main concern was that I'd stay for two years. I thought to myself, *Two years just gets you started.* I quickly gave them a four-year commitment with the provision that they allow me a summer sabbatical after four years. One of the things I had learned from my near-burnout experience at Walnut Creek in terms of renewal is that I needed to build a sabbatical into my schedule even before I took the job.

BEGINNING A NEW MINISTRY

When I began my ministry at Wheaton Bible Church, I struggled with comparison. I still do. Sometimes I wanted to preface my sentences with, "In Walnut Creek we did it this way," or "Out West we found this worked." It didn't take long to realize that the Wheaton staff did not want to hear about Walnut Creek. They wanted me to talk about what was happening in Wheaton.

In Walnut Creek our staff meetings were the highlight of my week. During those meetings, we ate lunch, told jokes, prayed together, and dreamed about the future. In Wheaton, I found the staff meetings to be very businesslike. Everyone sat around a big conference table with their calendars in front of them. In fact, coffee was banned from the meetings, and it appeared that little took place in the way of interpersonal relationships. It seemed to me that even the regular Sunday evening social gatherings were more formal among Wheaton staff members.

I had to come to grips with how I could make Wheaton be Wheaton and not Walnut Creek and God helped me work through the transition. With 11 pastors at Wheaton, the first major difference that I found between Wheaton and Walnut Creek was the size of the staff. Wheaton's staff consisted of three departments headed by the pastor of Christian education, pastor of development, and pastor of ministries. The pastor of ministries took care of visitation and counseling. The pastor of development took care of business, and the pastor of Christian education headed up children's, junior high, high school, college, and adult ministries.

As director of high school ministries, I felt as if I was being perceived as "the kid who works with high school students."

When a church goes through 7 youth pastors in 10 years, there are going to be image problems. There seemed to be no status attached to the youth pastor's position. It had been 18 months since a youth pastor had attended staff meetings because the interim youth pastors hadn't been invited to attend the meetings. I had a long way to go in terms of the image that the high school program had. Most of those youth pastors were recent Wheaton College graduates or had come out of the congregation. Therefore, they brought little new experience to the program.

In comparison, I was the first youth pastor who had a seminary education. Plus, I had been involved in ministry prior to my arrival at Wheaton Bible Church. I knew I was different, but the image that I was a kid who worked with kids bothered me. Chuck Wickman had warned me, "You won't enjoy *not* being on the upper levels of staff, Ridge." I have to admit that he was right. It took time for the church to understand exactly who I am.

Another major adjustment I had to make at Wheaton was to realize that the staff would be my colleagues, but not necessarily my friends. At Walnut Creek, my best friends had been the guys with whom I worked, especially the senior pastor. But I was told by a Wheaton staff member, "You will never have the same relationship with Wheaton's senior pastor, Chris Lyons, that you had with Chuck Wickman at Walnut Creek. Being from Boston, Chris is not as accessible because of his Eastern reserve."

My first few days on staff proved that out. The staff meetings were not run by Chris Lyons, but by our executive pastor. The senior pastor was strictly perceived as a counselor and preacher, while the day-to-day business of the church was handled by the executive pastor. I was disappointed that Chris probably wouldn't have time to get to know me, but the executive pastor seemed to have such an interest in the staff that I began to build a relationship with him.

Robanne had to make her own adjustments to Wheaton. At Walnut Creek, she had worked with student core groups and was actively involved in many aspects of ministry. In Wheaton, she was suddenly reduced to cleaning out my files. She was a great help to me, but I was really sad to see Robanne become almost directionless again.

Robanne had also taught preschool in Walnut Creek, but she wasn't sure that she wanted to continue teaching in Wheaton. Out of a desire to accomplish some of her personal goals, Robanne got a job as a preschool teacher at another church. It worked out well for us because her extra income allowed us to buy a home that we really liked.

I continued struggling with comparisons, and my comparisons turned into judgments. I began to compare Illinois with California. I missed hiking and backpacking in the mountains of California. While Walnut Creek is a fast-paced, cosmopolitan city, Wheaton is a very laid-back, conservative suburb. The "Christianness" of Wheaton was fairly evident to me. The Wheaton mindset seemed to imply that Christians who live here are somehow more spiritual than Christians around the country because of the centrality of so many Christian organizations in the area such as Wheaton College, Youth for Christ, Scripture Press. It even bothered me that Illinois roads had potholes and my car was beginning to show rust after the first few snowstorms. What had started out as simple comparisons had now become value judgments.

WHEATON STUDENTS

The biggest surprise of moving to Wheaton was how warm and accepting the students were. It didn't take long for me to fall in love with the students. I discovered that Wheaton students' priorities were different from those of California kids. High school plays, football, and other school activities played a big part in Wheaton kids' lives. Here the church was competing with the schools for kids' attention.

After one of the first Bible studies I taught, two seniors took Robanne and me out for pizza. During dinner, they began to share how they wanted the church to become more important in their lives and how they felt a little ripped off by the revolving door youth pastor policy. After that conversation, I decided to take an attitude survey like the one I had done in Walnut Creek. I called about 60 percent of the students, and asked them how they felt about Bible study, Sunday School, the senior pastor, retreats, and the youth pastor. As in Walnut Creek, most students were glad to hear from me. I discovered that most of the group loved Chris Lyons. They thought his preaching was relevant and that his skills in the area of ministry were somewhat directed toward them. At the same time the students were lukewarm about Sunday School. The one surprising factor was that they didn't like retreats.

On further investigation I discovered that practical jokes were ripping this group apart. There was a group of guys who were brutal on retreats. They enjoyed hurting other kids' psyches. They had gone beyond cornflakes in sleeping bags and plastic wrap on

---

THE NEW YOUTH PASTOR VS. CURRENT YOUTH LEADERSHIP

If you are a new youth pastor in a church with an existing youth ministry, carefully evaluate the current youth leadership.

First, observe why kids are acting the way they are. Ask yourself: *Why does the present leadership have some biases toward me?* It may have nothing to do with you as a person, but it may have something to do with your position. Students may feel as if they have lost power, authority, and status.

Second, observe who is standing on the fringes. *Who is waiting for new leadership?* Before you act, make sure that you have fully surveyed what has taken place in the youth group. Actively pursue answers to questions.

Finally, provide avenues for those who may be hurt by your new leadership. Be a listener. If those being hurt feel as if they're heard, some of the problems will be solved.

---

toilets to cherry bombing toilets and making certain kids slept outside cabins. I realized that one of the ways that I was going to make it with this group was through discipline and order.

As I began working there, I found that the student group was not healthy because only a small group of students had a great deal of ownership to the program. They felt strongly that they needed to preserve the program, so they were the ones who had worked the hardest to plan socials and run retreats. Some had even served on the candidate committee for the youth pastor. They had a strong position of power and influence over the rest of the group.

When I came in as a new youth pastor with a fair amount of authority and began to make changes, the kids who were the strongest leaders felt threatened by my leadership. The incident described in my journal is a good example of how students felt threatened by new leadership. Some of the students who had been humiliated or ignored by the current leadership of the group watched me closely to see how I handled the very things they had been dealing with during the past 18 months.

A power struggle arose between the kids who were perceived as leaders before I came and the kids who were chosen leaders after I arrived. The struggle manifested itself in my first summer mission project with the group. It was an inner-city project, and I selected the leaders. One student was part of the current leadership regime and one student was a "nobody" according to the group. Some of the current leadership regime felt slighted that I would bring in a new kid to run the trip, so none of the old power group went on the trip.

Minor problems began to surface as major deals. I chose "The Student Body" as a name for the youth group. As high school students who were part of the body of Christ, it was a good name to use. I then changed the name of the mid-week meeting, "Community," to "Body Life." While I felt the name changes were minor things, some students felt they were big deals.

For example, Body Life met in a basement of a neighboring house to the church, and I wrote a note one Wednesday night that said, "Body Life meets downstairs. Come right in." In response, one of the students crossed out Body Life and wrote in the word *Community*. At first, I was ticked. I thought, *How stupid and juvenile! Why can't they just cooperate?* But then I came to my senses.

I discovered that if my high school ministry was to be based on relationships rather than programs, it didn't matter whether I called the meetings Community, Body Life or Liturgy. If the kids felt loved, they would come. Therefore, I learned to be flexible, compromise on some cosmetic changes, and build relationships rather than fighting students on issues to which they reacted the strongest.

After having been in the Bible Church for five or six months, I met with four seniors to find out how I was doing. Bill Brown, Jim Jordan, Paul Negris, and Tom Peterson were the leaders of the program at this point. When I asked them how I was doing, they all looked at each other and grinned. "Ridge," said Bill Brown, "the very fact that we're here might tell you something. You're doing good." Bill didn't realize how important it was for him to say that to me. Once again I was being affirmed in my ministry by students.

WHEATON PARENTS

Wheaton parents were much different from families in Walnut Creek. They were incredibly concerned with what took place in their children's lives. At my first football game, I saw more parents than students—something that never took place in California. When I called my first parents' meeting, over 200 parents attended, and I began to see that Wheaton parents wanted to be more directly involved in the youth program.

It wasn't my style to have a great deal of parental control. In some cases, I felt that parents were not allowing students to make choices that they needed to make in order to grow up. For example, in Walnut Creek, we ran a college tour where all the students who were going to college visited seven or eight colleges representing different philosophies of education: a state school, a private secular university, a Bible college, a Christian liberal arts college, etc. I tried the same procedure in Wheaton, but it was not received well. To motivate their kids to go to certain schools, some of the parents asked me not to expose their students to other opportunities. In fact, some parents wanted to dictate that trip in order to have input on how their students reacted to certain colleges. I appreciated their involvement, but sometimes I felt that Wheaton parents were a bit more overprotective than California parents. Though I wasn't accustomed to this style of ministry, it was exciting to see parents that wanted to give so much help and assistance.

NEW PROGRAMS

Wheaton's youth program had some wonderful leaders. It was great coming to a program where there was strong lay support. For example, one core group leader, Linda Gerig, had worked with a small group of girls for four years through all the youth pastors and changes.

Early in my ministry, I surveyed my adult leaders to find out which areas of the program they believed the staff would consider optional. Having come from such a strong Mexicali program, I wanted to make sure that missions education came into focus on a regular basis. The church had a summer mission program called Project Serve. I was used to a spring mission project and wanted to duplicate the Mexicali experience in Wheaton. I went to Mark Senter and told him I'd like not to do Project Serve. "Ridge, this is one of those nonnegotiable things that *must* be done," he said. "You have no choice, you must do Project Serve." He felt it was intrinsic to the youth program, and the church would demand that I follow through on the project.

At first I thought, *I'll show him that I can make a better program during the Easter break than they've ever had during the summer.* Then I remembered that I needed to have a victory as I had at Walnut Creek. So I decided to make Project Serve that victory, taking what was already a very good program, expanding it, and making it better.

I was at a real disadvantage since Project Serve runs on a cycle, based on Acts 1:8. One year group members go to the inner city (Jerusalem); the following year to rural America (Samaria); and the next year to a foreign mission field (the uttermost parts of the earth). It was now time to minister in the inner city, which was perceived by the students as being the most uninteresting part of the program. And not only did I have to go to the inner city, but I had to go to Chicago, a local mission.

I found it difficult to motivate students to work in inner-city Chicago for two weeks, but a group of 23 students signed up to work at a rescue mission, teaching Vacation Bible School and holding evening services. Of all the mission trips I've taken, this was probably one of the most significant because we became a family. We learned to grow in our faith and our love for each other. We discovered the talents and abilities of each person. What I had felt would become a difficult situation became the very victory I was looking for.

Another area that promised victory was Sunday School. The students met in the cafeteria of a local junior high school because the church building was under construction. I began to do more and more teaching to express who I was and to establish myself as a good teacher. The students responded positively and the Sunday School grew. A sense of newborn confidence also grew in this group—more change than I was prepared for.

Times of sharing and community began to occur more often. When Sue Bolhouse, a freshman, barely missed being selected a school cheerleader, she shared her disappointment during one of our Sunday School classes. As she began to cry, a tenderness permeated the whole group.

However, there was still a group of students who were resisting leadership changes. At first I reacted by thinking, *Fine, I'll let them live in the past and I'll work with the underclassmen to build their leadership.* But God showed me clearly through guys like Tom, Paul, Bill, and Jim that these students were desperately looking for leadership, and that I needed to be their youth pastor too.

During my first year at Wheaton Bible, I had the only major student injury in my youth ministry experience. The Student Body was on a canoe trip about five hours down the river. We'd already portaged the canoe over two dams when I heard a scream. Paddling down the river, I came on a canoe where one of the guys in the group, Brad Hanson, had caught his finger in the eyelet at the tip of the canoe where the rope goes through. The canoe had rolled over and for all practical purposes, his finger had been amputated.

Some of the guys involved in the accident were the very guys who had been causing trouble on retreats.

First of all, I got Brad's finger wrapped and the bleeding began to stop. Then I packed in ice the part of his finger that was torn off and I felt could be saved. I didn't panic—I simply took control. But I was worried because I knew we were nowhere near civilization. We were at least an hour by car from a main highway. I thought, *This could be a 12-hour ordeal.*

Kathe Stoner, my canoe partner, and I got Brad in our canoe and began to paddle up river. We had to carry the canoe over a dam with Brad, who weighed about 220 pounds. When we reached the little dirt road that ended at the river, I left Brad and Kathe alone and began to run toward the main road which was at least an hour by car away. I'd been running about 25 minutes when I heard a car in back of me. I turned around and saw a police car with Brad and Kathe in the backseat.

We had prayed while we were in the canoe that God would send us help because we knew we were in a bad situation. I couldn't

---

OVERCOMING THE PREVIOUS YOUTH PASTOR'S HISTORY

When a youth pastor leaves a church, he also leaves a history. The only way that a previous youth pastor's history will go away is for the students to graduate. It takes four years until you are the only youth pastor that the kids will know and therefore, there's something to be said for longevity. As the previous youth pastor's history is flashed at you each year, remember that time is on your side.

A second way that you can overcome the previous youth pastor's history is through prayer. God knows that you have struggles in this area. As you begin to seek His wisdom on how to react to your predecessor, God will give strength and knowledge.

Another way to overcome your predecessor's history is to begin a new program or enhance an existing program in an area in which the previous youth pastor could not succeed. If there is no choir, start one. If there is no mission trip, plan one. In this way you can become distinctly different from the last guy because of your actions.

believe this policeman had just happened to decide to check out a report of a stolen canoe at that site and had stumbled across us. Because of God's intervention, the doctors were able to save Brad's finger and he has full use of it today.

The good thing about this experience was that the tough group of practical jokers began to view me as a leader. I became a person whom they could respect because I had appropriately handled an emergency. I don't think it was God's will for Brad to be hurt, but I do think God used that accident to establish me as a leader.

REMAINING FLEXIBLE

I discovered four ways to remain flexible during my first year at Wheaton Bible Church. First of all, I learned to develop patience in order to preserve unity (Ephesians 4:2-3). One of my main frustrations at Wheaton was with people who tended to forget that Robanne and I had a history. For example, when our anniversary arrived, people said, "Oh, is this your second or third anniversary?" They had no idea that we had been married seven years. Though we were 29 years old, we looked more like 23. They also seemed to ignore the fact that we had been through seminary and had four years of experience in youth work. While we weren't veterans, we were certainly experienced. It bothered me that people viewed us as kids, not as mature adults.

One of the ways Robanne and I showed people that we were an established couple with some stability in our lives was to hold an open house. About 200 parents came to our house one Sunday afternoon to check us out. Students helped serve refreshments, and every half hour I corralled guests into the living room to give a little talk about what the youth program was going to be.

It was also difficult for me not to think about what I wanted the youth program to look like three or four years down the road. I knew what the program would be because I knew who I was and what it would take to build a youth program. However, I needed to develop the patience to live one day at a time, build that program brick by brick, and preserve as much unity as possible in the youth group.

Secondly, I learned to build new relationships. When I arrived in Wheaton I looked for Delaynes and other people who resembled my friends back in Walnut Creek. But soon I realized that it took time to build those relationships. I found it particularly hard to do this at the staff level because I wanted affirmation right away. I learned to start relationships where people were, not where I wanted them to be.

When Jesus saw Zaccheus up in the tree (Luke 19), He went to him and said, "Let's go to your house and get on your turf. Let's understand who you are so that you can understand more who I am." That's a great example of the Zaccheus principle: Go to their house and see where they are. I can learn a lot about a kid and his environment by going to his house, seeing his room, and visiting his school classes.

The third principle for remaining flexible in a new ministry is to avoid talking about your former ministry. Students in Walnut Creek had given me a license plate that said "Flock 1." When I arrived in Illinois, I wanted to keep my California plates as long as possible since they were a curiosity-grabber. But after about two months, I realized that I needed to leave Walnut Creek. I got my basic Illinois plates and took off my creative plates. That was not only good for my image, but it was good for my ministry. I left the past and pressed on to the future.

However, I think you can learn from the past if you separate the principles and patterns from the people. I didn't find another Delayne in Wheaton, but there wasn't a Sue Bolhouse in Walnut Creek. No matter where my ministry is or what methodology I use, my programs amount to nothing unless the kids feel loved.

A fourth principle of flexibility in starting over is to develop new areas of ministry. This reminds me of Nehemiah, who was a very satisfied cupbearer to the king. But God gave Nehemiah a new ministry—to rebuild the walls of Jerusalem. He had to start looking for new and creative things to do in his new position.

One of the things I wanted to do in Wheaton was to duplicate what I had done in Walnut Creek. The problem was that students in Illinois and California were very different. So I began to investigate new avenues of ministry. Project Serve was one good stretching area. As God helped me recognize that I had to change some aspects of my ministry and relationships with the staff, I began to develop in my own spirit. Instead of viewing Wheaton as being different, I began to view it as an adventure for new ideas, dreams, and goals.

SMALL CHURCH SPOTLIGHT

PAM: Is it easier to be flexible in a large church or small church?

RIDGE: I think it's probably easier to be flexible in a small church than in a large church. In my situation with 200 kids, I can't really change the settings of my ministries. I'm limited as to the camps I can use for retreats because I usually need the whole camp. There are a limited number of things that I can do with 200 kids.

PAM: What are some practical ways to build flexibility?

RIDGE: Think of more than one way to do ministry. When you plan a retreat, plan it twice in a totally different form. For example, Project Serve was never run the same way twice in the six years I was at Wheaton Bible Church. One year we had one team that went to the inner city; the next year we ran three teams from three locations; the next year, seven teams from one location; the next year, a school of missions with one-week classes all summer long. It breaks your own traditions as well as the church's traditions.

PAM: Ridge, one of the problems with small churches is that we sometimes take the easy route. We get preset curriculum and prewritten programming, but that doesn't really take into account the need—centeredness of a youth group.

RIDGE: If I were working in a small church, I think I would try to plug into existing ministries that surrounded me, like camps or other youth pastors who do things very creatively and differently. Maybe use different resource people each year.

PAM: To meet the needs of my group, I've tried to vary my ministries. One year I took my group to a local youth seminar, the next year to a national youth convention, and the following year to a camp. But even though I've developed ways to make my ministry more need-centered, I sometimes have problems with recruiting staff members. **How do you deal with a revolving door staff?**

RIDGE: This is trite, but *don't quit.* God may have put you as a part-time volunteer in your church to be the anchor for the kids. I know that it's hard to retrain staff, but try to keep the perspective that the only stability this church may have for its younger generation is you.

eight

CREATE IN ME
VISION

WEDNESDAY, *April 4*

Today Project Serve was run by two students, Sue Bolhouse and Thom Day. Sue and Thom really believed that our misson teams could make a difference here at Pineywood High School. I had my doubts. We had been told that the high school kids in this rural area of Mississippi would be disruptive and hostile toward northerners, particularly white northerners. Actually, we were scared, afraid that we would fail. Prior to our arrival, a group of students who had tried to minister in this area had been so harassed that they left the school crying.

Sue and Thom decided that we should organize this project in such a way that we spent a good amount of time in prayer today concerning the ministry at Pineywood. So, this evening all 75 students came back from their individual projects a little bit early to spend some solid time in prayer.

Evening came and we loaded the buses and vans to go to Pineywood. We arrived on campus and found the black students a little unfriendly toward us. We filtered into the huge auditorium and introduced the sports movie we had selected to show. Over 400 students got unbelievably quiet as the film started. Each testimony in the film was greeted with silence until Chicago Bears' Walter Payton came on the screen, cutting through tackles in order to score a touchdown. The auditorium erupted as guys stood on their chairs giving each other high fives. The students applauded, screamed, and cheered as Walter did his thing. Then as #34 gave his testimony, the place became quiet again.

At the conclusion of the film, I was sort of planning to be run out of town, but Sue and Thom looked at me as the silence continued. I decided to stand up and give an invitation for students to receive Jesus Christ. We were totally unprepared for what took place. Student after student came forward. We had no Bibles. Many team members were not trained in how *to lead a kid to Christ.*

As I gave the invitation, I put each kid with one of my students who could explain the plan of salvation and pray with him. Something fantastic happened as students were given an opportunity to lead another kid to Christ. Suddenly, my students saw that Ridge Burns was not the only person who could minister. They began to see that God could work through Sue and Thom—and them as well!

WITHOUT VISION, youth ministry is boring. Students enjoy doing things that are exciting and creative. That's one reason why music videos are so important to kids right now. They take the kids to another dimension.

In youth ministry, we need to take students to another spiritual dimension. Kids need to be placed in risky situations where only God can work. That's why they like to go backpacking, climb out on the edge of a cliff, and give you a heart attack. They enjoy the feeling of doing things that are different and wild.

But in youth ministry, we have substituted craziness for vision. We bring in an electrically—wired stool, or a Christian rock band, or the world's largest banana split because we know students will say, "Yeah, that's crazy enough. Let's do it!" We make our mistake in limiting kids to our zaniness when we could give them a vision of turning a community over for God. In this chapter, I am going to share how I learned to delegate my visions as well as my creative enthusiasm to students.

STUDENT DREAMS

During this year I was amazed at how God used the high school students at Wheaton Bible Church to motivate me to dream. Because of their spring experience in Mississippi, Sue Bolhouse and Thom Day began to dream bigger dreams and see obstacles as opportunities to do bigger things for God.

Thom attended a public high school, and was sort of a macho/cowboy-type, big on soccer, and a natural leader. He was deep on organization and very confident. Sue, on the other hand, was a preppie dresser from a Christian high school. She was very tender, and we could make her cry by telling her something sad. Both of these students loved the Lord and were filled with an intense loyalty to the Student Body.

I asked these two sophomores if they would again help lead Project Serve. By this time, Project Serve had become so large (65 students) that it was not appropriate for us to go as a large group to any more sites. We had increased the population of Mendenhall, Mississippi by 10 percent, and we didn't feel that was an adequate missions experience.

For the next Project Serve, Sue and Thom decided to break the whole group into smaller groups so that we could accomplish more for God and provide students with a better cross-cultural missions experience. They came up with a plan to take three simultaneous trips in different directions, all leaving on the same day. One team went to New Hampshire to work in a church connected with an organization called His Mansion. Another team went to Denver, Colorado to work in a small inner-city church. The third team planned to work at a camp in Galapa, Colombia.

We selected four other students to help lead the three teams. I met with these six students every other week for a whole year as we planned the programs, fund-raisers, and ministry opportunities. On the day of departure, we commissioned 80 students on the platform of Wheaton Bible Church. I remember feeling proud and nervous. I was proud because the students were dreaming a bigger dream—each student had more responsibility in the mission experience. At the same time, I was nervous about delegating and relying on a staff of student leaders.

I'd never spent much time really thinking about how to delegate more in order to accomplish more. Boxed in by my time and space requirements, the program had been limited to what I could physically do in 24 hours a day, seven days a week. Suddenly, because of Thom and Sue's vision to do these three simultaneous trips, our program became much larger. Students were taking more and more leadership.

After the commissioning service, we went over to a house where the three teams ate dinner together. I stood on the street corner and watched two vans drive off to New Hampshire and two vans head for Colorado. I was going with the team to Colombia for the first few days, then circulating to each site before the projects were completed. Suddenly, near-panic set in as I realized that the program was out of my control. *What if someone gets hurt? What happens if all the planning and arrangements at the sites don't work out?* It was a difficult moment for me, but it was exactly what God needed to bring into my life to help me understand the meaning of delegation.

When the Colombian team arrived in Barranquilla, the strange culture hit us right away. Going through customs, I sensed a real nervousness in the kids—almost a giving up of their American rights. Most of the students had never been out of the United States. I was nervous too, not about going through customs, but about giving up some rights I had as a youth pastor to the students at the two other sites. When we left the air-conditioned airport terminal, we were overwhelmed by the heat and humidity of the tropics. It was terribly hot as the adult sponsors and I began to load luggage and materials on a flatbed truck for the 45-minute drive to Galapa.

We arrived at the site and the student leaders began setting up camp. There was just one problem—me. I had a hard time letting students lead and found myself mentally clinging to ownership on the Colombian site. It took a long time for the students to be able to function with me there.

For example, when the student leaders announced we would eat dinner at 5:30 P.M., I thought, *Why didn't they talk to me about that?* As a youth pastor, I felt I should be in control and make sure every decision was approved by me. Our plans were to run Vacation

---

ADVANTAGES/DISADVANTAGES OF A PROGRAM BEYOND YOUR CONTROL

Advantages:

1. You are able to provide a bigger program that's not contingent on your time/space requirements.

2. You provide more student ownership. Students must take leadership in the program when you don't have the time or abilities to pull it off.

3. It increases your delegating abilities.

4. It improves your relationship with God in terms of relying on Him to do things that are beyond your control. It puts you in a position of exercising faith and taking risks.

Disadvantages:

1. You begin to feel isolated. Your job becomes more administrative and less ministry-oriented.

2. It requires that you have a well-trained, loving staff. If the staff changes, and you've created a program that requires a good staff, you may be in trouble.

3. You have less involvement with students, in terms of kids' personal lives.

Bible School during the week, take the weekend off, and then do another ministry the following week. The problem was that our schedule didn't fit into the situation in which we found ourselves. Instead of consulting me about making a change in schedule, the student leaders took charge and made a decision to set up a better schedule.

After several days, Thom Day came up to me and said, "You know, Ridge, this trip is going to go a lot better when you leave." I thought, *Why is Thom saying this to me?* I was really hurt at first, but then I realized I had no role on this team. The adults, students, and site leaders were doing *their* jobs. *Ridge,* I said to myself, *Project Serve ends for you when the students leave Wheaton. The best way for you to lead students is to allow them to make their own decisions and then help them work through problems.* So on my last day with the team, I finally got my act together and began encouraging the students.

As my time in Colombia came to an end, I prepared for the arrival of our senior pastor, Chris Lyons. I had invited him to visit the site, because I wanted Wheaton Bible Church to catch a glimpse of my vision for Project Serve, and I knew Chris would be a spokesman to the church. It was a great opportunity for me to build a relationship with Chris and for him to understand what the students were doing. I met him at the airport and took him to the site. He was very impressed, and I was excited to see his support and willingness to spend time with me in South America.

From Colombia, Chris and I planned to spend a weekend in Ecuador visiting some missionaries. It was tough to leave the students in Galapa. As I waited for a bus to take Chris and me to the airport, I went over to Thom Day, put my arm around him, and prayed, "Lord, protect this team, and run it through Thom." It was almost like turning the keys of your new Porsche over to a brand new driver. I watched his countenance change as he took on responsibility and realized that I believed in him. What a lesson for me to learn! After almost seven years as a youth pastor, I had finally learned how to trust students and give them authority to make decisions.

As I got ready to board the bus, Karen Stoner, the other student leader, came up to me and began to cry. She thanked me for allowing God to work through her and trusting her with this responsibility. There were adult leaders present, but I had turned the keys of the program over to Thom and Karen. For the first time I realized the students didn't need me to lead; they needed me to motivate, and I could best motivate them by leaving the site.

I sat quietly on the bus as we rode into town. Instead of trying to ask what was wrong, Chris quietly patted me on the shoulder and said, "I understand." He knew when to leave me alone and let me sort things out.

From Colombia, Chris and I flew to Ecuador to visit missionaries at radio station HCJB and then down to a little village called Shell. From there we flew into the jungle. Indians surrounded the plane

BUILDING A RELATIONSHIP WITH THE SENIOR PASTOR

Building a close relationship with your senior pastor is important because:

• He is usually your boss. Remember that since he's your boss, you need to submit to his authority. A close friendship can contribute to that boss/employee relationship.

• He may be nervous about the power that a youth pastor has. When the youth pastor commands the interest of the young family and speaks with authority on how parents can handle problems with their children, the senior pastor may become nervous.

• He may be lonely. Being the person in charge may be a tough position. Your senior pastor may simply need a friend.

• He may be looking for someone to disciple. Make yourself available, not by forcing him to disciple you, but by building a friendship that will grow into a discipling relationship.

Here are some ways to build a relationship with your senior pastor:

1. Take him out for coffee on a regular basis.
2. Schedule a weekly luncheon with him.
3. At the beginning of the week, review his sermon, explaining the parts that are most meaningful to you.
4. Write him notes of encouragement.
5. Make a sign for his door regarding some event in his life such as completion of a class, birth of a child, or return from a vacation.
6. Ask him how you can help him on a regular basis.
7. Always speak highly of your senior pastor to your contemporaries, staff, and students.

as it taxied down the landing strip. There we met Rachel Saint, sister of Nate Saint who along with four other missionaries was murdered by Auca Indians in the late 1950s. Rachel offered to take us down the Curaray River in some dugout canoes to the site where the five missionaries were killed. When we arrived at the site, Chris went off by himself. I could tell that he was emotionally moved by the experience of standing in the spot where five people died because they believed in Christ.

I sat down on a rock at the site of the martyrs' deaths and tried to visualize myself landing in a small plane in a totally unreached area with potentially hostile people. I thought, *What would it be like for Robanne to allow me to do that? Would I be willing to give my life for God? Would I be a martyr, or would I make excuses?*

As I sat there reviewing my life, I thought about how easy a full-time youth pastor's life is. I had a respectable salary, a healthy budget, a good staff, and efficient facilities. Yet, there were five men who sacrificed all these facets of life to share the Gospel, knowing they might be killed in the process. Quietly recommitting myself to the Lord, I wondered if I would ever have that kind of spiritual fortitude.

When I saw Chris again I realized there was no need to tell him about my experience. I think he knew that something spiritual had happened to both of us that day.

In Columbia I discovered that I need time away from the kids so I am forced to trust God in order to be personally renewed. It seemed funny to be so physically apart from the students and yet feel so much responsibility for them. I was finally able to trust God to protect them.

SUE'S DREAM

About a month after the students returned from Project Serve, I had a long talk with Sue Bolhouse, one of the leaders of the Denver inner-city project. Sue went with me to drop Robanne off at the airport for a trip to California. On the way home, Sue looked over and said, "Ridge, I'd really like to do something big for God. I started to dream in Denver about accomplishing something, but I don't want to wait another year. What can I do? How can I dream on?"

I didn't have a dream for Sue at that time, but I thought, *Now there's a highly motivated student. Let's see what she and I can dream!* Another thing that crossed my mind was, *Oh brother, what am I going to do with this student?* It was almost a bother. I knew if I didn't see a dream in Sue, I would have to manufacture a dream for her and that would make more work for me.

Sometime later, I remembered seeing a slide show about three years prior to my conversation with Sue. It showed an area in south Carol Stream, Illinois about a mile-and-a-half from our church that had some high-density housing. I had heard that the apartment complexes in that area were full of children.

Because Sue's Denver project was primarily working with needy kids in the inner city, I thought, *Why don't we see if we can start a program to help children in Carol Stream?* Remembering my days at Westmont College when I had participated in a program called Sidewalk Sunday School, I wondered if we could develop a similar once-a-week program to help the Carol Stream kids.

I picked up Sue one day and we went out to the Carol Stream apartment complexes. At the rental office we asked if there was a community building that we could use to house a Sidewalk Sunday School. It just wouldn't be possible to run the program outdoors during the Chicago winters.

Our talk with the rental agent revealed that crime was a problem in this community, so I called the police chief of Carol Stream and asked where he would like us to work. He suggested one particular complex that had 1,200 residents with 200 children under the age of 10. One hundred twenty of these kids were "latchkey children." That was a new term to me, but I discovered that it designated children who are left unsupervised before or after school by their parents or guardians. Most of the parents don't like the situation, but because of economic strains on the family, they have to leave the children alone.

As we left the rental office, we were told that no community building existed. The only way we could run this project was by renting an apartment for $375 a month. Sue looked at me and said, "There's no way that we can come up with that kind of money." We both knew the church would not support the program at that cost.

Driving through the complex, we saw a school bus letting off children. It was at this point that I was struck by the critical need. Suddenly, I experienced some of the same emotions that I felt on my world trip to Thailand, India, and Hong Kong. In much the same way, my heart was pierced as I saw little kindergartners get off the bus and reach into their shirts and lunch boxes for keys. I realized that most of these children would be waiting all afternoon for their parents to come home.

Sue looked over at me and asked, "Ridge, why are you crying?" "I don't know," I replied. "This just really makes me sad."

"Ridge, we've got to make a difference here," said Sue. At that moment, we decided to claim the apartment complex for God. First, we claimed it through prayer, asking God to lead and direct us as we worked with the residents. Secondly, we claimed the complex as our specific mission field, and finally, we determined to take our ministry to that area to do whatever it took to be Christ in that community.

Our first obstacle was raising the money needed for the apartment. We would need at least $6,000 a year to run the project. We thought about doing car washes and fund-raisers, but then Sue came up with an idea.

"Why don't we just take a collection? Why don't we just tell the rest of the Student Body the need and see what they can do financially?" suggested Sue. So we decided to go on a faith program. We asked students to consider giving $1.00 a week to Sidewalk Sunday School.

After giving our report on the apartment complex, we asked the students to pray about the project. When the day came to collect pledge cards, more than 100 students turned in pledge cards that totaled over $700. We had reached—exceeded—our goal for the first month!

Sue began to dream on. She went out to the apartments on a regular basis to play with the children. I worked with the management of the complex while Sue built rapport with the kids. Whenever she walked through the complex, kids called out the windows, "Sue, hang on. I'll be right down. I want to talk to you." Sue began to be very much respected by the community.

We signed a lease that committed the Student Body to a year of ministry at the apartment complex. Sue organized her peers so that a student staff was ministering each day. We decided to start out working three days a week with a big brother/big sister program. Soon we had more than enough staff to run a combination Vacation Bible School/tutoring program. We met the kids as they got off the school buses and took them to our apartment where we sang, played games, worked on crafts, told Bible stories, and memorized Scripture.

On the Sunday before we started the program, we loaded up three buses of high school students and took them out to the apartment complex. We crowded into the rental office and held a dedication prayer service. I talked about how the children of Israel marched around the city of Jericho seven times in order for God to do His job. Symbolically, we claimed the complex, praying that God would bless our ministry.

On the first day of ministry, Sue and I got together to pray. We took the high school student staff out to the complex, not knowing whether any children would turn up. The first day, 28 kids came and Sidewalk Sunday School was born not because of my vision, but because I allowed God to use students to accomplish His work. The entire project was started by one 16-year-old girl who had a big dream for God.

We began to run a five-day program. Other churches wanted to get involved, so we let two other churches in our area take on some summer ministry. Sue began to fall in love with the project. She motivated 60 of her fellow students to minister each day at the complex. She divided those 60 students into teams so that each day had its own staff and each staff its own director. Sue then met with her directors and accomplished most tasks through delegation. I began to see that Sue was doing the same thing that I had learned to do.

During this time, discipleship was taking place. Sue and I met to pray, study God's Word, and plan Bible stories for the Sidewalk curriculum. Instead of going through a discipleship curriculum, Sue and I began to share our lives together as we ministered at the apartment complex—sort of a "moving discipleship." I began to realize that I could disciple kids by motivating them to dream and then helping them to accomplish those dreams. I had shifted my responsibilities from controlling students to making them reckless for God within spiritual limits.

It was a joy to see students' hearts broken as they began working with abused children and dealing with situations God wanted for their lives. For example, Pete Talbot, a football player for a local Christian high school, came in my office one afternoon and said, "Ridge, I just took a kid home from Sidewalk Sunday School and saw a family with no furniture in their apartment except a Coleman stove and mats." Parents of students like Pete would call me after their students returned from the apartment complex and say, "I don't know what's happening to my kid at Sidewalk, but this has really affected his view of God and how he relates to our family."

Sidewalk Sunday School started to be noticed by the community. A local Christian TV station decided to do a feature on it, and Christian publishers began to interview Sue. I was amazed that when they called they wanted to interview me rather than Sue, so I began a policy that I would only be interviewed with a student who was participating in the program. It was very difficult for me to convince publishers and the media that it was not my program, but the students' program.

Not long after we launched the program, *Guideposts* magazine presented Wheaton Bible Church with its Church of the Year Award. I was especially excited because Sidewalk Sunday School was the factor that helped us capture the award, and I believed the program deserved recognition. Getting the award meant we would be featured in a national magazine and a public relations firm from Park Avenue, New York would arrange for a major media event in Chicago.

On the day the award was to be given, a press conference with over 40 journalists was held at the church. By this time, Sue had graduated from high school and was a student at Biola University in California. We flew her back to receive the award on behalf of the students who were currently running the program. I said a few words, and Dr. Norman Vincent Peale spoke, but the media knew who the real hero was when Sue got up and told her story.

The next day, Sue's story ran on the second page of the Chicago *Sun-Times*. Sue getting the award from Dr. Peale . . . Sue being interviewed on radio and TV shows. . . . Two years earlier that would have bothered me. But I had learned something. Youth programs aren't run for youth pastors; they're run for students. And the real stars are the students whom you can motivate.

I was so proud of Sue and her successor, John Diehl. Throughout the media blitz, Sue stood in front of TV cameras, radio announcers, and newspaper reporters, testifying about who Jesus Christ was to her, and how she had not started Sidewalk Sunday School for her own glory, but to uplift Jesus Christ. Sue had discipled John, and when his turn came to be interviewed, he too clearly presented the Gospel. Once, when John and I were speaking about Sidewalk on a Chicago radio show, a lady called in asking, "Why do you give up your afternoons to work in this program?" John answered, "I do this because this is what God has called me to do. I want Jesus Christ to be first in my life, and I want people to know that." His answer showed me that high school students can say far more than I can about what God is doing in their lives.

LEARNING TO DREAM

One of the most important principles I have learned in youth ministry is to dream dreams so big that only God can make them

**WHY CAN'T THEY JUST MOW THE LAWNS HERE
AT THE CHURCH THIS SUMMER?**

come true. Not being afraid of failure is one of the keys to dreaming. By putting myself in positions where there is potential for failure, I have learned to rely on God—like Moses when he tried to persuade Pharaoh to let the Israelites leave Egypt. Moses put himself in a position where he was ridiculed and persecuted. He also knew that he was going to take a trip that was nearly impossible if Pharaoh let the people go. The potential for failure was great, but Moses' vision for the Israelites' freedom was fulfilled by God who gave him that dream (Exodus 3—14).

In the same way, Sidewalk Sunday School could have been a total flop. We could have taken a step of faith and had no kids show up for the after-school program, or we could have been evicted from the apartment, or the Student Body could have ignored Sue's dream. But God worked in the hearts of the apartment complex residents, the Student Body, and the Sidewalk Sunday School leadership to fulfill Sue's dream.

A second principle in learning to dream is to ask God to give you a dream. As Sue and I began to explore ways to accomplish great things for God, we first asked Him to direct our thoughts. Sue's dream came as a result of a vacuum created in her life. My dream for Sidewalk Sunday School began when I saw resident children getting off the bus. Just as it was no accident for Moses to meet God at the burning bush, it was no accident that God allowed me to be at that corner when those children came off the bus.

A third principle in learning to dream is to allow others to make mistakes so that you can perform ministry. When Peter, in his exuberance, tried to meet Jesus as He walked on the water, he learned a strong lesson about the cost of taking his eyes off the Lord (Matthew 14:22-36). I think Jesus allowed Peter to sink in the lake in order to teach him this lesson.

Similarly, there are times when I am dreaming or leading others in dreaming when mistakes can be turned into learning experiences. When I first arrived in Colombia, I found myself constantly wanting to rescue the kids. One of the lessons I learned from my Colombian experience is that if I really want to delegate and teach kids to dream, I cannot be a rescuer.

A fourth principle in dreaming is to trust God to work in others and create visions for them. In Mark 3:13-15, Jesus chose the men with whom He wanted to share His life and dreams. After their training, He sent out the disciples to preach and have authority over demons. As a youth pastor, I've learned to choose a group of adults and students with whom I can share my dreams and train them to be visionaries. Both Sue Bolhouse and John Diehl are examples of student visionaries in my life.

Learning to dream also involves a fifth principle of seeing obstacles as challenges that permit dreams to come true. When Moses led the Israelites out of Egypt he probably thought, *How am I going to feed them? What will I do about discipline? How will I take this many people on such a long trip?* God probably responded to Moses' questions by pointing out that He could make miracles out of those obstacles. In the same way, as I dream and take risks, I want to continue to see obstacles as opportunities for God to work. For example, I want to see the Student Body's winter camp not as a normal retreat, but as an experience designed for 100 kids to learn more about Christ. Another obstacle is the facility at Wheaton Bible Church. I would prefer small group Sunday School classes on Sunday mornings, but our facility won't allow for this. So, instead of having Sunday School in its traditional setting of small group studies, I have created a youth rally atmosphere. Then the room becomes an asset, and that's what I mean by dreaming my way out of obstacles.

A sixth principle in dreaming is to disciple others to catch your dream. My students will only dream if I'm a dreamer. Paul says that "Whatever you have learned or received or heard from me, or seen in me—put it into practice. And the God of peace will be with you" (Philippians 4:9). When I dream, my students mimic what I'm doing. If I want students to catch my dream of building a house in Appalachia, I must take them to Appalachia so they can experience the need for homes. Kids will catch the dream if they run alongside me for a while.

When I first got out of seminary I thought I had to be a great teacher or a good musician or a talented administrator to be a successful youth pastor. Though I'm sure a youth pastor needs to be able to speak with authority, I've never felt that I was a powerful teacher or speaker. And I don't think programming is one of my strengths. Rather, I believe that God has given me the ability to envision things that few others see.

This year helped me determine exactly who God wanted me to be. I realized that I didn't have to meet the expectations that people seem to place on youth pastors. Rather, I could be who I am—a visionary—and be successful.

HOW TO START A SIDEWALK SUNDAY SCHOOL

Approximately 4-6 million children under the age of 10 come home from school every day to an empty apartment or house. They get off the school bus, let themselves into their homes, and watch soap operas for the rest of the afternoon. Sociologists indicate that the "latchkey" problem will grow, and by 1990, it will become the leading social problem of our society. Sidewalk Sunday School is a daily cross-cultural experience where high school students can counteract the latchkey problem and, at the same time, experience missions in their own backyard. Following are steps to starting a club in your community.

STEP 1—Select a student who can catch your vision to be the spokesperson for the ministry. Students listen to other students. If you want your whole group to participate in Sidewalk Sunday School, find a student who can transfer his vision to his peers.

STEP 2—Investigate the vision. Call your police chief and get information about the high-density housing districts, poverty areas, and cross-cultural situations in your community. Check with the county departments to see if any research has been done on the community in which you plan to minister. Obtain information from county health services and schools attended by the children. Share specific information about the latchkey problem, the research results, and the costs of a Sidewalk Sunday School program with your students.

STEP 3—Provide your group with a biblical base for their ministry. Teach your students about widows, orphans, and the responsibilities Christians have to make suffering peoples' loads lighter.

STEP 4—Pray on a regular basis for this mission. Pray that your vision will spread to your entire group and that their hearts will be broken by the needs of latchkey children.

STEP 5—Set a specific day to enlist group support. Ask students to make a three-month commitment to give up 2 ½ hours each week to work in the program.

STEP 6—Select a site by determining the size of your program. A high school group of 200 students can handle about 60-70 latchkey kids. A youth group of 15 can probably handle only 5 students. You may choose to minister in an apartment complex or in a residential home depending on the size of your group.

STEP 7—Organize your students for a "hands-on" leadership experience. Select a student director for each day that Sidewalk Sunday School is in operation. The diagram below illustrates how each director is responsible for staffing and motivation.

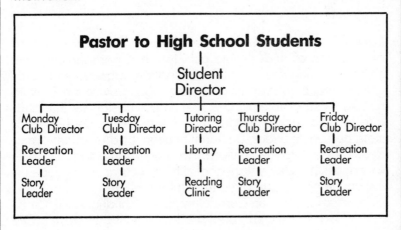

Pastor to High School Students

Student Director

Monday Club Director	Tuesday Club Director	Tutoring Director	Thursday Club Director	Friday Club Director
Recreation Leader	Recreation Leader	Library	Recreation Leader	Recreation Leader
Story Leader	Story Leader	Reading Clinic	Story Leader	Story Leader

PRACTICAL CONSIDERATIONS

Insurance: Make sure you have adequate liability coverage. Ask your church to select an insurance committee to handle special problems.

Lease: Get permission from your landlord to hold classes and activities associated with Sidewalk Sunday School on the premises. Below is a sample agreement letter.

Re: Agreement

We the undersigned agree that the _____ Church will be holding "Bible Study" type classes at _____ different times during the week. The undersigned acknowledges this fact and agrees that any liabilities that occur in the home are not to be held against the Real Estate Corporation.

Signed,

_____

_____

_____

Legal Considerations: Guard yourself against any kind of suspicion of undesirable activity. Child pornography and child molesting are possible allegations against your program. Hire a lawyer to give you legal advice on how to handle these problems. Get written permission by the landlord to hold such a program on his property. Require each staff person to wear an identification badge at all times. Require the latchkey children to wear name tags.

Curriculum: Use a variety of different curriculums depending on the age group of your latchkey children. I recommend Character Foundation Curriculum, Early Childhood Kit, Christian School Curriculum, published by Fleming H. Revell, Old Tappan, New Jersey.

A TYPICAL DAY AT
SIDEWALK SUNDAY SCHOOL

3:30 P.M. Staff meets at the church to pray together, and the day club director gives a thought for the day

3:45 P.M. Staff arrives at the site, puts on name tags, and sets up five interest centers; playdough center, storybook center, household center, building center, and puzzle area

3:55 P.M. Staff waits on the street corner to meet the children as they get off the school bus

4:00 P.M. Staff begins recreational activities and interest centers

4:30 P.M. Group singing

4:50 P.M. Bible story

5:05 P.M. Memory verse and craft time

5:25 P.M. Closing prayer; staff members walk kids home and return to the site about 5:30. Then they have a 10-minute prayer session before returning to the church

6:10 P.M. Return to the church

CROSS-CULTURAL GUIDELINES

Because you are sending students into a cross-cultural situation, not only in terms of race and language, but also in terms of economics, instruct your students to follow this list of guidelines:

1. Do not give your address or phone number to any resident at the Sidewalk Sunday School site.

2. Wear your Sidewalk Sunday School badge at all times while on Sidewalk Sunday School premises.

3. Be careful about your relationship with the opposite sex.

4. Do not accept gifts from Sidewalk Sunday School participants.

5. Do not enter any other home except the Sidewalk Sunday School residence.

6. Follow this dress code:
No sweat pants.
No T-shirts with questionable advertising or messages.
No sandals. Shoes should always be worn.
Avoid immodest dress.
7. Avoid comparisons between your culture and the people you find at the site.
8. Be friendly. Greet everyone you see, and be sure that people understand that they are welcome to your program.
9. Do not hang around your peers. You are there to serve the population.
10. Walk kids home only in pairs, never alone.

THE DIFFERENT PROGRAMS IN SIDEWALK SUNDAY SCHOOL

Tutoring Program—Contact local elementary schools and ask for training assistance in tutoring programs for latchkey children at your Sidewalk site. Focus on reading, math, and writing skills. "Homework Helpers" should attend training sessions directed by professional tutors.

Library or Reading Club—Begin a program in which church members can donate old children's books. Then open a library or book club at your Sidewalk site where children can check out books. If a kid reads 30 books and writes a book report, give him a Sidewalk Sunday School T-shirt.

Sports League—Have some of your athletic students organize team games such as basketball, indoor soccer, or floor hockey for older latchkey children.

Latchkey Choir—Get parental permission to bring your latchkey children to your church. Kids love to sing and your church will love to hear these children.

Food Drive—From time to time, ask church members to donate canned goods. Create a food pantry for needy families at your Sidewalk site.

Adopt-a-child—Assign each latchkey child to a church family. Ask each family to pray specifically for their child. This provides a great link between the latchkey family and the church family.

SMALL CHURCH SPOTLIGHT

RIDGE: Pam, is it easier to delegate your visions to students or to adults in your church?

PAM: To students because they don't ask so many questions, they just do their jobs. Adults sometimes have a hard time seeing the whole picture. But kids don't feel a need to see the whole picture. They just work on their part and know the dream will come true. However, I have to resist telling kids what I want them to do.

RIDGE: Dictating dreams is just one of the problems with being a visionary. Another problem is that you occasionally steamroll students. There are some kids who don't want to dream. Another drawback is that visionaries don't see the students anymore; they only see their dreams.

PAM: How do you prevent that from happening?

RIDGE: I build a staff that cares about the students, and I try to sow seeds of my visions in the kids.

PAM: What happens if you don't have highly-motivated kids or high achievers?

RIDGE: Then you need to build a vision on the students' level. It would not be a big deal for my kids to paint their Sunday School room. But that may be a challenging task for a small youth group. Your visions have to be in proportion to the motivation of your students. But don't underestimate your kids.

PAM: How can a volunteer or part-time youth worker motivate his students?

RIDGE: Trust them. It's the same principle that a business has when hiring a student. An employer gives a kid a drawer of $1,000 and says he wants the money back at the end of the day. Most kids are motivated to do the right thing. Sometimes you have to prove to students that you trust them. For example, on Project Serve if I tell a kid to find the cheapest air fare to Colombia, I don't turn around and make the same phone calls to the airlines to check ticket prices. Once the student sees I trust him with this task, he catches the vision and runs with it.

PAM: And if he doesn't follow through on the task?

RIDGE: There has to be a penalty. I allow him to look bad in front of his peers. That doesn't mean I embarrass him, but I let his own actions embarrass him.

PAM: And do you trust him again after he's failed?

RIDGE: Yes. It's not easy, but I do.

PAM: You talk a lot about visions you have had for large churches, but **what kinds of visions can a youth worker have at a small church?**

RIDGE: Bigger isn't better. Any youth group can have a vision. Trevor Ferrell, a junior high kid, had a vision to feed the hungry of Philadelphia, and he has been very successful. It's a matter of breaking out of the constraints of youth programming. If we taught geometry the same way that we teach theology, the kids could never do math. There is no laboratory; all we do is lecture all day long. Vision brings a sort of laboratory experience.

PAM: One of the problems in a small church is that kids can have a larger vision than that of the church. Some small churches are small because the parents or adults have a small vision and don't want a large church. In some ways, the kids' visions can be stronger than the adults'.

nine
CREATE IN ME
INTENTIONALITY

MONDAY, January 22
Robanne came home really disappointed today. She was so excited when
she started the preschool at Wheaton Bible. Under her leadership as founder
and director, the school had grown from 40 to about 100 children in two
years. Now there was a need for a kindergarten, but the board at Wheaton
Bible Church turned down her proposal to start a kindergarten.

The board is pleased with her work, but they feel the school is consum-
ing too much of the building. "It's crowding out other valuable ministry op-
tions like the women's ministries, refugee classes, and other daytime pro-
grams," they told her. That's a good reason, but it doesn't change the fact
that Robanne's dream was killed today. She's frustrated, and I don't even
know how to encourage her because I'm discouraged about my job as well.
We've almost reached a state of boredom in our ministries and our mar-
riage—a maintenance mindset.

INTENTIONALITY IS AN AREA that many youth pastors don't
quite know how to handle. They think about motivation and
creativity, but they don't think about the need to be purposeful
about what they do. Many youth pastors float from program to
program. They go to a conference, hear a good idea, and try it.
Then they read a magazine and try something else the next week.

Youth pastors try all these programs because they think they'll be
successful. Without clear goals, they end up going through programs that they think will work, rather than designing programs
that will meet the real needs of students.

Intentionality helps a youth pastor resist the tendency to have a
maintenance mindset in his ministry. A maintenance mindset oc-

curs when a youth pastor loses his ability to dream. He starts looking at what *is* rather than what *could be, reacting* instead of *reaching out.* In this chapter, I'll share how a maintenance mindset affected my work at Wheaton Bible Church.

RIDGE'S MINDSET
In my third year at Wheaton Bible Church, I learned that maintenance and preservation can bring discouragement. The previous year, the church had won national awards and gotten a lot of media attention. I had been excited to see students catch the dreams of Sidewalk Sunday School and Project Serve.

But for every reward there is a reaction. Some segments of the church, including students and staff, reacted negatively to the awards, media attention, and platform time that was given to my visions. They thought, *Should a ministry get an award and all this recognition?*

It was also interesting to see how youth groups operate in leadership cycles; not every class of students is equal. When I first came to Wheaton, we had a very strong senior class. When they graduated, I lost a lot of leadership from the group. But during the next year, the junior class became incredibly strong as they grew spiritually, and desired to serve God in some creative ways.

In spite of the spiritual growth of the students, something was wrong in my life. Both Robanne and I had reached an impasse in our ministry—a maintenance mindset. At the same time, our marriage felt a little stale. We had now lived in the same house for four years and were beginning to talk about having to redecorate. Prior to Wheaton, we had never stayed in one home long enough to have its carpets cleaned. Even our cars were beginning to show some rust because they had gone through several Chicago winters. All these things were symptoms of our not creating a dream, and they reflected our maintenance-oriented personal lives.

I was not in a good state of mind. Robanne was struggling with her own goal in life, whether or not we should have children, and how we should be involved together in ministry. Her dream of starting a kindergarten had been shattered by the church board, as mentioned in my journal. Yet my youth ministry was going well. The dreams that Sue Bolhouse had started with Sidewalk Sunday School and Project Serve were being blessed by God. However, my own life was destitute.

My maintenance mindset had several results. First, I started to meddle in things that had nothing to do with high school ministry.

For example, I was irritated with the cleaning service that took care of our church, so I continually voiced my opinions about the kinds of supplies they used to shampoo the carpets. I had an opinion about everything—the church bulletin, van maintenance, computers, landscaping. I was disturbed about where people were parking and not parking. I was obsessed with burned-out light bulbs. It's no wonder I created some *conflict*, which is the second result of a maintenance mindset.

As staff conflicts became more frequent, I became a sort of lightning rod for staff complaints. Fellow staff members really struggled with my work style and the incongruity in my organization of my ministry. Soon they began to take shots at me personally rather than just criticizing my ministry. Comments like, "The students really don't like you, Ridge." "The only reason the kids are coming is because they like your staff." "Ridge, you never get serious" began trickling into conversations.

I was accused of running over people in order to get what I wanted. My mission trips are one example of how I unknowingly steamrolled staff members. A sense of power comes with the involvement of 90 to 100 kids in overseas missions, so I had the power to work within the system or break the system. Since I was on a power high, I didn't bother to fill out the business department's forms or follow necessary procedures. I just charged full speed ahead.

Everything about me seemed to generate conflict: my growing close friendship with the head pastor, the facts that I drove a pickup truck, lived in a condominium, and didn't have children—my whole lifestyle. Robanne and I felt we didn't fit into the perceived Wheaton mold where people move to the suburbs and live quiet lives. We didn't want our lives to be quiet; we wanted to go against the wind.

Consequently, the third result of my maintenance mindset was defensiveness. Someone would ask why the high school students didn't attend the evening worship service, and I would elaborate on how the service did not meet students' needs. I would never have been so negative if I had been dreaming bigger dreams. With a maintenance mindset, I didn't control my tongue very well. My budget hearings were terrible; I spent my time being overly defensive about my programs, saying things more strongly than I meant. The problems weren't all mine, but I helped cause them by forgetting that ministry is servanthood—the opposite of defensiveness.

Another result of my maintenance mindset was that I hoarded

RESOLVING STAFF CONFLICTS

Unresolved staff conflicts can paralyze a ministry. Try to apply these four principles to conflict situations in your ministry.

1. Keep the account clear. Believers are encouraged to "seek peace and pursue it" (Psalm 34:14). Don't let offenses and wrongs pile up without righting them with your associates—support staff, pastoral colleagues, and secretaries.

2. Keep your office door open. A pastor's life should be one of open transparency. What is said behind closed doors is often more intense than what would be said in the presence of others.

3. Make sure you have a well-written job description and are reviewed on an annual basis. Often the reason for staff conflicts is an unclear job description or an undefined role. These organizational conflicts can be resolved through clearly communicated job descriptions.

4. Try to have a quarterly staff sharing time. Ask each staff member, "How are we getting along?" This gives each member an opportunity to share honestly how he feels.

supplies, space, power, and visibility. If there were five pieces of poster board in the church media center and I needed one each week, I would take all five to make sure my needs were covered for five weeks. Knowing that my actions caused some inconvenience for the staff and teachers, I stockpiled supplies. At this point I was building my own kingdom, not caring about others' needs. As I became more defensive about my budget, I made sure to hoard certain things that would assure my success with programs and ministry.

In hoarding space, I found myself scheduling meeting rooms with no real plans to use them—but just in case I wanted to use them. That created real conflict between the buildings and grounds department and me. I also abused the power of accessibility to the church building by making a point of being in the building at weird hours. Though I had a set of keys, I must have set the church alarm system off 20 times during the year, bringing the police to the premises each time.

I wanted visibility so I made sure to be on the platform a lot during Sunday morning services. I would sacrifice sitting with high school kids in order to sit on the platform.

When I was with other youth pastors, I found myself strutting, a fifth result of my maintenance mindset. I made sure that my peers knew I was writing a book, involved in speaking, going to elders' meetings, and leading the largest youth group in the area. Why those guys kept accepting me, I'll never know.

WHEATON BIBLE CHURCH'S MINDSET

The Wheaton Bible Church had just completed a $5 million building program, and the congregation in general was also in a state of maintenance. Having accomplished their dream of erecting the building, they were now feeling the "post-building blues"—cloudy and sluggish.

Bureaucracy became a real part of the Bible Church. Because we were a large church in a new building we felt that we needed to impose certain business structures, authority structures, and organizational structures—all of which began to eat at me. There were forms to be filled out every time I mailed a letter or dialed a long distance phone call. Making a purchase required seven documents—a purchase order, a requisition, a computer-generated requisition, and copies to several people.

Even our church offices were indicative of a maintenance mindset. They were located on the building's third floor. A visitor walking in the front door would find a large atrium with no signs and unlit halls. After finding his way to the third floor, he would discover a well-organized machine that took care of a very large church. The problem was that we weren't easily accessible to the church, and when we appeared inaccessible, people didn't come to us with their problems. We ended up running more and more programs, thinking we were meeting people's needs, but remaining too isolated.

The bureaucracy just reinforced my maintenance mindset and filled my heart with a low-grade rebellion. More and more, I felt our church was involved in itself and not in its people. That whole mindset spilled over into my youth program, core groups, Project Serve, and Sunday School.

I became inaccessible to kids for counseling and spent less time meeting one-on-one with students. On Wednesday nights, when the kids arrived in the atrium, all the core group leaders were down there, spending time with them, trying to integrate themselves into the students' lives. I, on the other hand, was usually still in my office, working on a program with one or two students, talking to an adult staff member, or figuring out room assignments for core groups. Unless I had an agenda, I spent very little time with students.

In the past I had investigated the possibility of having Sunday School on Sunday night and not even having a high school ministry on Sunday morning. Such creative ideas were replaced with questions like, "How can we make Sunday morning better?" and "How can we all fit in the same building?" While these replacement ideas were still creative, they were not goal-directed and intentional.

Because I had just taken the church from a high school budget of $2,000 to a budget in the neighborhood of $35,000, there began to be real tension between the business department of the church and the ministry department. As I experienced more budget hassles, I found myself spending increased time defending my expenses to the finance committee. There was never a doubt that I was financially trustworthy, but there was suspicion on the part of the finance committee that the church wasn't getting its money's worth in ministry.

People began to question how much things cost. "Are we getting $35,000 worth of ministry out of the high school department?" they asked. Project Serve became a friction point because people wanted to know for certain that they were getting what they paid for from the program. I had to justify all my programs based not on what was taken out of the church budget, but on the gross expenditures of a particular event. For example, our winter retreat cost a total of $15,500, an amount partially funded through student fees. The net cost to the church was about $3,500. When the finance committee began to talk about gross numbers instead of net, they looked at the retreat as a $15,500 gross expenditure. Some felt that if parents didn't give their money, we would be running a rather expensive high school program. The finance committee's logic was that if the parents didn't spend that money on the high school program, they would still give it to the church for other purposes.

I know I was a real source of irritation to the executive pastor and the business department because I didn't fit into their mold. I didn't fill out forms and talked flippantly about the business department. I began to compare the dollars spent on the high school program to the dollars spent on other church programs. I fought about my philosophy of youth ministry. No doubt the financial committee was frustrated when they weren't able to accomplish some of their goals because of my insensitivity to them.

STAFF MINDSET

Because I was one of the more visible people on staff, as well as being closely associated with the well-publicized Sidewalk Sunday School, I began to get too much attention. Some staff members felt I was out of touch with the rest of the church; they didn't understand that I sometimes did unusual things not to be different, but to reach for the cutting edge of youth ministry. As the staff started asking some legitimate questions about my ministry, I began to withdraw.

Many staff changes were under way. Naturally, in a church with 12 pastors, somebody is always coming or leaving, and seniority is very important. A pastor's position of influence may not be based on his skills so much as his longevity. At this point I had seen all but 3 of the church's 12 pastors come on staff. As I became one of the senior members of the staff, tension and conflict arose.

Taking on a bigger role in the church, I appeared on the platform more regularly and was very much involved in the worship planning of the church. My relationship with the senior pastor really began to develop. We spent a lot of time together, mostly at the office, very seldom socially. We bounced ideas off each other and began to really disciple each other. It was a good experience, but as this relationship became more visible to the rest of the staff, I became isolated and lonely. It appeared to me that the staff began to consider me a threat since I was receiving more platform exposure, had direct access to the senior pastor, and was branching out beyond the "youth" area.

CULTIVATING INTENTIONALITY

Struggling to overcome my maintenance mindset, I discovered that I needed to be more intentional in accomplishing ministry. Four courses of action seemed to be helpful; the first required seeking honesty in my current relationships. One day, Wheaton Bible's director of support services came into my office and said, "You know, Ridge, you are really, really strong in what you do. You are one of the best high school pastors I've seen. But when you're bored, you meddle."

At first, I thought, *Come on, that can't be right.* But the more I thought about her words, the more I realized she was right. God really spoke to me through this staff member as she shared these verses with me: "Do not repay anyone evil for evil. Be careful to do what is right in the eyes of everybody. If it is possible, as far as it depends on you, live at peace with everyone" (Romans 12:17-18).

BELIEVE IT OR NOT, A LOT OF WORK AND PLANNING WENT INTO THIS.

What she was basically saying is, "Mind your own business." In 1 Thessalonians 4:11-12 I found that my ambition as a Christian should be to lead a quiet life, mind my own business, and watch my behavior in front of non-Christians.

During this time Chris Lyons became my best friend. We spent hours together dreaming about what the church could be and how we could get it there. We discussed ideas about how to be better ministers. Eventually, we made a covenant to meet every Friday for lunch and just talk about all kinds of things, church included. As we talked openly and honestly, I began to see Chris as a caring person who has some of the same needs and struggles that I have.

Another relationship on which I worked was my own marriage. The church graciously allowed Robanne and me to take a six-week sabbatical during the summer. Part of that time we spent in San Francisco, and instead of flying home to Chicago, we took a train. For two-and-a-half days we sat facing each other, talking, sharing, and dreaming together. I fell in love again with Robanne in a special way as I began to realize what a great person God is making in Robanne and how she is a perfect complement for me. Her self-control and stability rub off in my life and help me smooth down some of my rough edges.

The second course of action I took to get out of my maintenance mindset was to develop other ministry interests. At Pentecost, Peter addressed the crowd saying, "Your sons and daughters will prophesy, your young men will see visions, your old men will dream dreams" (Acts 2:17). It seems to me that God is asking the people to look to new horizons and keep dreaming. Therefore, I became involved in developing the South Carol Stream Project which expanded Sidewalk Sunday School. We tried to get an ecumenical movement together to establish a counseling center, head-start program, and medical relief for the Carol Stream area. As a member of the steering committee, I was able to externalize my ministry and become involved with a whole new group of friends. If I couldn't dream at the church, I could dream somewhere else.

Another ministry interest developed through the opportunity to work on this book. I thought, *Maybe I've got some things to say that can help other youth pastors when they're in this mindset.* This creative outlet seemed to be a good way to apply my skills and creativity.

My third course of action for moving forward in my ministry was to cultivate relationships with the pastoral staff. In Matthew 22:34-40, Jesus gave His disciples two imperatives for relationships. One is to love God with all your heart and soul and mind (Matthew 22:37), and the second is to love your neighbor as yourself (Matthew 22:39). I could not continue in ministry until I looked at how I was handling the relationships in my life.

One of our elders got together with me for lunch one day and said, "Ridge, you've got some fence-mending to do if you want to survive in the church. No one's going to fire you. You're strong and your ministry is going well, but there's a lot of talk about how you've hurt people. How are you going to resolve this?"

So I went around to the offices and made sure that I said hello or had a cup of coffee with the other staff members. Boy, did I find the walls up! I *did* have a lot of fence-mending to do! Some of the staff couldn't even see that God was alive in my life. While I was excited to see what God was doing in my own heart, the pastoral staff couldn't see it. I had unintentionally hurt some staff members, who thought I did not care at all about their programs and ministries.

For example, Project Serve gained so much notoriety in the church, it became a threat to our missions director. For some reason, she began to think that Project Serve was a liability rather than an asset to her program. I wanted her to have more authority, so I kept saying the missions department ought to oversee Project Serve, while she argued that it should be overseen by the Christian education department. That conflict was finally resolved by the elders, but I had to spend some time with her to heal our relationship. I apologized to other staff members for steamrolling incidents, and God did a unique healing within our staff.

One relationship on which I worked was with Rick Trautman, then Wheaton Bible Church's pastor of junior high ministry. Rick became my Timothy. I made sure that we spent a little more time together. I introduced him to some of my friends, and began to help him understand his ministry. Wanting to pour my life into him programmatically, I began to pray more directly about Rick's ministry. I felt as if we were coworkers in ministry—not Paul, the big guy, and Timothy the guy who needs to learn—but Paul and Timothy who ministered and worked together as a team.

Returning to the basics was my fourth course of action in moving my ministry forward. I discovered there are certain basics that a youth pastor needs to provide to students in order to have an effective ministry. *In Search of Excellence* by Thomas A. Peters and Robert H. Waterman (Harper and Row) lists 10 characteristics of a successful company. One of the characteristics is that successful companies stick to what they know they can do best. My problem was I'd gotten involved in a lot of activities that did not reflect my main skills.

In Paul's letter to the Ephesians, he notes that believers are joined and held together in growth and maturity as each part does its work. I finally realized that I was trying to do the work of the whole body of believers and not just the part that God had called me to do. Part of the reason I was in a state of maintenance was because I was too involved in a lot of externals. Sidewalk Sunday School, retreats, coaching golf, and playing basketball with the guys were not the primary ministries I was called to do. I wasn't called to be a coach, a basketball player, or director of a latchkey program. I was called to minister to high school students at Wheaton Bible Church by building up my staff, teaching the Word, and providing a contact with kids.

I learned to focus on goal-setting, my mission statement, and accessibility to my students. So I became more personally involved in the basic youth program on Wednesday nights and Sunday mornings. I assigned myself a core group of students to work with one-on-one. My Sunday morning teaching became alive and students began to respond to the Word. To my surprise, even the staff began to come on Sunday mornings, because they were also being ministered to by my teaching.

GOAL SETTING

Setting goals and writing objectives are absolutes for youth pastors. Without a clear focus for ministry, a youth pastor will begin to feel directionless, and eventually take on a maintenance mindset. Following is a sample outline of responsibilities, goals, and objectives that I produce each year of my ministry. Use this format to develop your own goals and objectives. Then share your ideas about the direction of your youth ministry with your pastoral staff, board, volunteer staff, and students. You may be surprised at the difference goal setting can make.

HOW I SEE MY JOB

Position: Pastor to High School Students

Reports to: Senior Pastor

The purpose of the job of pastor to high school students is to provide overall direction for the development of the high school students of the church for the purpose of introducing them to a relationship with Jesus Christ and assisting them in maturing in their understanding of how this will impact on their future. It is the function of the pastor to high school students to assist the students in understanding their role in the church. The ultimate goal is the preparation of lives for future service to Christ.

RESPONSIBILITY	GOALS	OBJECTIVES
I. Pastoral Ministry to High School Students	1. Core group ministry.	To increase the number of core groups to 30, having 150 students involved each week in small groups.
	2. Personal contact with the students of the Student Body.	To make five contacts a day for the purpose of spiritual encouragement to individuals of the Student Body. That encourgement can be done through a letter, phone call, or a visit to a student on campus.

3. High visibility on the high school campus.

To attend at least one high school event a week on campus—plays, football games, soccer games, high school assemblies, etc.

4. Accessibility and counseling.

To schedule and communicate clear office hours to the Student Body and parents.

To be available for crisis counseling with families.

5. System of accountability for students.

To have each core group leader write behavioral objectives for their students and keep accurate records on how those objectives are being met in the students' lives during the school year.

6. Mission or service opportunities.

To continue the growth of student leadership by running a Sidewalk Sunday School and Parents Club on a regular basis.

II. High School Staff

1. Recruitment, training and discipleship of adult staff.

To meet weekly with the Student Body adult staff for prayer, fellowship, and planning.
To be involved in actively recruiting *new* adult staff.

To provide some kind of service opportuniities for the adult staff so they are growing in their faith as they lead students.

To provide adequate training stimulus for the adult staff.

2. Recruitment, training, and

To meet weekly with a team of students who

	discipleship of student staff.	are working to accomplish a task goal for God.
III. *Curriculum Development*	1. Need-centered curriculum	To survey students' needs to develop a need-centered curriculum.
		Allow core group leaders to select their own curriculum based on the needs of their core groups.
		To provide an accurate and active monitoring process for core group leaders.
	2. Doctrine-centered curriculum based on the needs of general spiritual development in adolescents.	To require each core group leader to produce quarterly lesson plans for his core group.
		To teach in an expository fashion one book of the Bible.
	3. Service or mission experiential curriculum.	To expand Project Serve to include an overseas experience next year.
		To support, direct, and encourage the expansion of Sidewalk Sunday School.
IV. *Planning*	1. Long-term goals.	To provide a monthly newsletter called the *Screamer* for parents and elders so people are aware of what is going on in the Student Body.
		To have this year's Student Body calendar approved by the Christian education committee,

		the pastoral staff, and the Board by May.
V. *Staff Relation-ships*	1. Staff support and encourage-ment.	To allow the music pastor access to the Student Body for musical education.
	2. Resource person in high school ministries.	To provide resources only in the high school area and stick to my own business.
		To build my relationships with the staff by spending time alone with staff mem-bers.
VI. *Personal Manage-ment.*	1. Personal strength and develop-ment.	To participate in the Mexicali program in Mexicali, Mexico during Easter break.
		To read books that will stimulate my understand-ing of the high school cul-ture.
		To continue writing to ex-pand my ministry to national publications
		To be involved in a per-sonal time management reassessment so I can do things more efficiently with less time.
VII. *General Church Involve-ment*	1. Exercise the gift of faith in promotion and public relations in the church.	To be available to the senior pastor and assist the general church in its growth under his direction.

SMALL CHURCH SPOTLIGHT

RIDGE: How important is intentionality for you as a part-time person, Pam?

PAM: I can't begin to describe its importance. Let me describe a week at my church without intentionality.

Saturday: *What can I do tomorrow morning for a Sunday School lesson? It's almost Easter, so maybe I can have the group look at Jesus' last week in Jerusalem. Or did I do that last week?*

Sunday: *I'd better prepare tomorrow night's Bible study.*

Wednesday: *I wonder if anyone remembered to buy refreshments for the youth group meeting.*

Thursday: *Almost forgot to stop by the hospital and see Kim.*

Friday: *One of these afternoons I have to decide where to schedule the spring retreat.*

RIDGE: My week would be practically the same. For a full-time volunteer, a maintenance mindset can be disastrous. A small church's expectations may be fairly nondescript, but one or two kids in a small group can put a lot of pressure on the volunteer to go in the directions of their needs. However, those directions may not meet the needs of the rest of the group members. Intentionality is particularly important for the part-time person because he can easily end up burning himself out, going on tangents.

PAM: Are there any other keys to intentionality besides the four plans of action mentioned in this chapter?

RIDGE: Servanthood is a key. If I want to be intentional about meeting students needs, I must first be a servant. I must also allow myself to be interrupted by students and staff, whether it's the kid who is working on building and grounds or the sponsor dropping by to discuss a problem.

PAM: With only 12-15 kids in my group, servanthood for me may be showing up at a freshman volleyball game for the 33rd time, writing a letter, or taking a student out for pizza.

Do you think the basics for ministry are the same for a large church as those for a small church?

RIDGE: I think they're exactly the same. You've got to have an active Sunday School that helps students understand their faith and supports the worship services. You also need some sort of small group synergy where kids feel they are being ministered to on an individual basis. But most of all, there must be some structure or program where the kids feel loved.

ten

CREATE IN ME
INTIMACY

TUESDAY, March 18

Today, Rick Trautman asked me to come into his office for coffee. As we told jokes and talked about our ministry, I decided to risk a little more intimacy with Rick.

"Rick, I'm restless," I told him. "I've been here almost five years, and now I'm praying about whether or not to leave Wheaton Bible Church." After I told him I was thinking of leaving, Rick began to share with me how important I was in his life and ministry. We talked about the ministry ideas we have worked on together. It was exciting to remember all the things God has done through us.

I don't think Rick was cognizant that he helped me recall exactly what my position is here at Wheaton Bible—to pastor high school kids. God worked in my life today through Rick.

IF THERE IS ONE COMMON INGREDIENT in good youth pastors, it is intimacy. The successful youth pastor finds a group of people with whom he can be intimate and vulnerable. For me, that involved a small group of students with whom I was working on a task. But it also involved a group of adults.

Once I made myself vulnerable to these people, they began to see me not just as a leader who could solve youth ministry problems. They also saw me as a person in process who is trying to serve God by learning more about Him. Then I was perceived more as a servant than a dreamer.

The successful youth pastor must commit himself to a group of people on a regular basis. Then he must learn to share his life with those people. This chapter will explain how I developed intimacy in many areas of my life and ministry.

INTIMACY WITH THE STAFF

After a year of maintenance, God worked in my life to drive me into building more relationships with people. One reason I was feeling bored with my ministry was because I was too involved in programs and not involved enough with people.

I began to build some great relationships with our church staff. Rick Trautman, our junior high pastor, and I had become good friends during my year of maintenance. With all the criticism that went around with some of the staff changes, Rick and I had a common bond of working more intensely with students than some of the other staff members. We went to conferences and began spending more time together socially. Even our wives began to build a relationship.

Though Rick is eight years younger than I, he began to be not just a person who came to *me* for ideas, but a person I could use as a sounding board. Rick doesn't get very excited or emotional, so he had a very mellowing effect in my life. He helped me react more effectively to other staff members. We'd get out of a staff meeting, and I'd say, 'Do you believe that we have to fill out more forms to

---

THE "MINOR LEAGUE" TRAP

Many times high school pastors view junior high pastors as working with the minor leagues. By keeping junior highers in your ministry mindset, you will view them as appropriate ministry opportunities. To avoid prejudicing yourself against junior high ministry, try the following ideas for junior high involvement.

1. Spend time working with junior high students. Often you will find them more responsive than you first anticipated. Go on a retreat with the junior highers. Have your high school kids throw a party for the junior highers.

2. Pray through the enrollment list of the junior high department. View those kids as the future high school ministry and pray consistently for those students.

3. Write the junior high students notes of encouragement on their birthdays or other special occasions in their lives. Surprise them by telling them you're praying for them.

secure rooms in the church?" He would respond, "Ridge, don't be such a jerk; just fill out the forms. They're not that big a deal." I could run into his office with a great idea, and he would be able to help me analyze that idea determining its good and bad points.

I began to see more of Ridge Burns appear in Rick Trautman-type programs. He began to look at his programs and evaluate them based on their creativity and ability to minister to students. He also began to develop good staff relationships—modeled, I think to some degree, on what he saw happening at the high school level. Even my creative flair for graphics began to influence Rick's retreat fliers and brochures.

I think I had fallen into the trap of seeing junior high ministries as the minor leagues of high school ministries. Rick changed all that as I understood his goals, dreams, and visions.

Another person with whom I continued to develop intimacy was Chris Lyons. We not only continued our weekly Friday lunches together, but spent more time just talking about the church, our families, and world concerns. Sometimes we'd just sit down and share burdens together. I could say things to Chris and they would roll off his back. Then I wouldn't feel the urge to say them to anybody else. I would complain about what I was feeling and Chris would give me a new perspective. It was my relationship with Chris that helped me grow.

I also began to build a relationship with Rod Jones, who lived in our Sidewalk Sunday School apartment since the large corporation from whom we rented would not allow us to rent an unoccupied apartment. Rod was looking for something to do for one year, and I asked him if he'd be one of my interns. He raised his own support and for a year we worked together. That relationship was built on common experiences with students. Rod was able to relate to a whole new group of students to whom I didn't relate.

A great listener, Rod loved to work with disinterested and apathetic kids. God used him to help a core group of guys who were really struggling with the institutional church. These fringe students started dreaming bigger dreams because of Rod's ability to dream with them. Rod and I spent hours in my office talking about the one-on-one strategies needed to meet those students' needs.

I also set a goal to develop the volunteer people we call the associate staff. This year I decided not to recruit adults based on their ability to work with students, but on whether they expressed an interest for deeper relationships and were willing to become part of a synergetic team of leaders.

Because we became a team, we began to spend a lot of time together. One night we were sitting around a table, talking about what we had for the previous night's dinner. One couple had peanut butter-and-jelly sandwiches. Another guy went to the deli. Another guy didn't eat supper. Another person ate leftovers from his neighbor's refrigerator. The 28 of us decided to get together every Tuesday night for a potluck supper. It was a big time commitment, but we found that we were people who didn't eat well and needed to just eat a good meal together and have fellowship.

Though the group didn't naturally fit together—the associate staff was made up of a man in his 50's, newlywed couples, single adults, and several moms—members had a common thread of love for high school students and a need to get together for fellowship since for various reasons we didn't fit into our own peer groups.

The Tuesday night potluck became my family time, the church meeting I most looked forward to. No set agenda, no big preaching, not a lot of prayer. But a fellowship of spiritual intimacy. There were times we would talk so seriously it was almost scary. We discussed our spiritual responsibility to our parents as young adults. *What do we do if our parents are living carnal lives?* we asked ourselves. *What is our view of money, the church, our devotional lives?*

There were tears and hugs. There were also times when we were so interested in watching a TV miniseries that we didn't do anything but sit around and watch TV. But that's OK because we were a family unit.

One of the associate staff members was Suds Seelye, a four-year core group leader who had worked with the same group of girls since they were freshmen. She recently watched them graduate, and began to feel something that was brand new to me—core group withdrawal. *Should I give her a new group to automatically replace the group of girls who graduated?* I wondered. She had built such intimacy with these girls that it was hard for me (or her) to imagine starting at square one. Not wanting to lose her contribution to the program, I gave her an "intensive care" job where she could spend time ministering to students who just didn't fit in.

Megan Kelly and Mary Hamm are two great young teachers who work with the Student Body. Professionally, Megan Kelly works with learning-disabled students. She loves to make cookies and encourage others. She began to open her home every Friday night so students could watch "Miami Vice." Fifteen or twenty students would come over to eat Megan's cookies and watch TV together.

SELECTING A VOLUNTEER STAFF

Three basic requirements should be considered in choosing a volunteer staff to work with high school students.

1. Recruit people who are team workers. Many people in a church would be excellent leaders in the high school program, but some may not work together well with the existing staff. The students are very aware of problems in an adult staff, so choose staff workers who can develop relationships with each other.

2. Recruit people who model the Christian life for students. On high school campuses, the teachers most respected by students are not necessarily ones fresh out of college. They are people who have built a sensitivity to students and committed a lifetime to working with high school students. Too often in churches we recruit a staff from those who are the young and immature.

3. Recruit people who are spiritually alive. A volunteer staff needs to have answers for students' problems. People who are spiritually walking with God and have a daily prayer life provide consistency in a high school program.

Maybe it's not the most highly polished youth ministry, but my program has little value unless the students feel loved. And Megan loves students. To have 20 students meeting at somebody else's house, building relationships with her, would have been threatening to me five years ago. Now that's exactly what I want students to do. They're building relationships with each other and with my staff, so the ministry is bigger than my personality and my time/space requirements.

Mary Hamm has a burden for a rest home ministry. She began to take students every Sunday afternoon to one of the local rest homes. Now she has 10-12 students involved each week. I have never been involved in the rest home ministry, but it was fun to watch how God worked in Mary's life as she began to minister to the students.

All these staff members have used different methods to develop intimacy. Suds used longevity and developed so much intimacy with her students that when they graduated from high school and Suds' core group, there was a vacuum in her life. Megan built intimacy by having kids in her home. Mary developed intimacy with her students by doing a task with them. Intimacy, I learned, does not have to come just from me; students can be intimate with each one of these leaders. My job is to develop intimacy with each member of my associate staff.

INTIMACY WITH STUDENTS

The difference between this year and any other year in my life was the depth of my relationships. My students were developing intimate relationships with me and my staff. For instance, Gail and Ralph Sweatte have been core group leaders for three years. Recently when Gail went through some major surgery, it was exciting to watch her core group love her and care for her. While she was in the hospital, her core group would find someone to drive them there. Then they would sneak in and have their core group meeting in Gail's room. They felt this was the best get well card they could give her. Obviously, students have a ministry to adults, just as adults have a ministry to students.

I continued my relationships with students. My friendship with Delayne Roethe grew as we continued to write back and forth. One summer I spoke at Mount Hermon, California, near Delayne's home, and we picked up right where we left off. The principle of encouragement that I had seen in Delayne eight years ago was still alive in her life. She was still a dreamer, even though her diabetes had made her slow down a bit.

Sue Bolhouse and I continued to build our relationship. I remember when Sue left for Biola University. I wasn't looking forward to the day. She was going to the airport at 5:30 A.M. I got up early and drove over to say goodbye to her. Being the emotional type, I was a little afraid of what was going to take place. After she loaded up her car, we said good-bye and prayed together. As I drove off in my little blue pickup truck, I thought, *It's the Sue Bolhouses that make me want to stay in youth ministry.*

Shortly after she got to Biola, Sue wrote me a letter. I had written her a letter and put it in her carry-on bag for her to read on the airplane. Her letter read something like this:

Dear Ridge:

The airplane ride was good. Your letter made me cry. Taking off from Dad and Melissa was really good. The only other time I cried was when I read your letter and when I landed in L.A. But I'm stuck here now. Please pray I like it, Ridge. I miss you.

I hurt now. Please pray that I will get better. I'll call tonight.

Sue

It's hard to read that letter now because there are all kinds of tear stains on it. I don't know if I've ever had a relationship with a student quite like the one I've had with Sue. She was a great dreamer, and she taught me so much. I was pierced by her letter. I could understand her hurt because I hurt also.

In lots of books and sometimes in seminary, I was told not to get emotionally involved with students, particularly if they are females and you're a male. Yes, you have to be very careful about the kinds of relationships you build, but in this case, it was important for me to be part of someone's life who needed me. Too many times I have been so involved in programming, and not in students' lives, that I heard no one saying, "I need you."

Another lesson in student relationships came through Project Serve, which had a new twist for me this year. Meg Larson and J.T. Bean were chosen as student directors. They were responsible for seven of their peers who were site directors. I worked primarily with the two directors and they interpreted what they learned from me to the site directors. It was a great system. It forced me to be responsible and accountable to students in a new and different way.

We decided to take a trip where we would all sleep, eat, and worship together. Then each of the seven teams would have their own ministry site and go out each day to minister. Meg and J.T. were responsible for the overall program while the seven site leaders were responsible for the daily programs. Meg, J.T., and I met every Thursday night for almost a year to discuss, pray, and share about Project Serve. The longer we got together, the less time we spent on Project Serve and the more time we spent on building relationships with each other.

The administrators of Mexicali, Ron Cline and Carolyn Koons, had asked me to be the dean of the Mexicali camp—run all the chapels, handle discipline problems, and basically manage the 3,000 people coming across the border. I decided to take Meg and J.T. with me to Mexicali, and then go on to Ensenada to check out the Project Serve site. We were able to spend 11 uninterrupted days of ministry and travel together. What that did to our relationship was unbelievable.

One night as we drove back from Mexico, Meg slept in the back seat as J.T. and I talked. As J.T. shared with me his goals and dreams of becoming a youth pastor, I realized he had been watching me from the moment I got up to the moment I went to sleep to see how I reacted to certain situations.

In the middle of that conversation, we talked about some of the sins that prevent us from having a great relationship with God and how we could keep alive our relationship with God. I thought to myself, *Maybe this is the reason why the disciples seemed to be such a close-knit group. They traveled and spent time together.*

Meg was different from J.T. in that she was a program-oriented person, a perfectionist as well as a dreamer. She loved to plan events with everything lined up in the proper order before the event took place. Number one in her high school class, she has impeccable morals and a vibrant spiritual life. Yet with all that going for her, I sensed Meg wanted a bit more out of life. So I gave her the dream of running Project Serve.

The problem with Project Serve is there's no way to have all the details planned down to the minute. Relationships, people, and the Mexican mindset all get in the way. Three days after arriving in Ensenada, Meg was depressed—not because her plans weren't working, but because her site leaders had done their jobs so well that she didn't have any role. With nothing to do, she felt bypassed and friendless.

One night after everyone had gone to bed, I went by Meg's RV. Her light was still on so I knocked on the door. "Meg, you're not happy, are you?" I asked. Meg prides herself in always being in control, but that night she burst into tears. I put my arms around her and she cried and cried. I thought, *Meg is finally to a point of being broken before God, and I am privileged to be a part of that. She is finally in a position where only God can move.* "Ridge, " she said, "I can't do it, only God can make this trip successful." Meg was finally giving the trip to God. From then on, those tears became an indicator to Meg of God's working in her life.

I learned that relationships make the difference in youth ministry. It's the relationships that keep me going. It's also the relationships that get me criticized for favoritism. After all, only two people could be Meg and J.T. Students would say, "I'm not Meg or J.T. They're your favorites! You're not spending time with me!"

To counteract that criticism, I began to write notes and letters. My goal was to write 20 encouragement notes to different members of the Student Body each week. Handwritten notes are a tough job for a youth pastor, but I am always amazed when I visit a home and a high school kid takes me to his bedroom. Pinned up on his bulletin board, I see my short notes like "Hey, you're a star!" or "Hey, you're great!"

INTIMACY WITH MY FAMILY

My relationship with Robanne took some different turns this year also. Having been married 11 years, and both being 34 years old, we decided we should really take seriously the question of whether or not to have children. Robanne was discouraged with her job and really wanted to change her life. Her ministry at the church pre-school was winding down, and she was not building friendships with her contemporaries. In fact, she would say, "Ridge, I'm not going to live next year like I'm living this year. I need a new dream."

I had met with Ron Cline, president of HCJB radio station in Quito, Ecuador when I was in Mexicali that year. We had the kind of relationship where we could really talk about the directions of our personal lives. He was concerned that we would regret not having children after we were too old to have them.

"Ridge," he said, "you can trust God in every other matter of your life. Why don't you trust God to give you children if it's His will? And if you're not supposed to have children, He will prevent conception from taking place."

After praying and thinking about it we decided to take Ron's advice. We stopped using birth control on February 1, and that very day Robanne became pregnant.

Our whole lives started to shift, not only in terms of relationships with students and the staff, but now in terms of family. Our intimacy increased as Robanne and I spent hours talking and dreaming with each other. We had to work on cribs, changing tables, and painting the house, so I took a little time off work and fell in love with Robanne even more.

On October 24, 1985 Ridgeway William Burns III was born. I went home from the hospital and wrote him a letter. As a youth pastor, I thought I'd better talk to him about relationships.

To: Ridgeway William Burns III
    To be opened on October 24, 1998

You came into my world this morning at 11:39 through a lot of pain and a lot of work from Robanne, and you announced your presence with one of the sweetest sounding cries I have ever heard. As I held you for the first time, I wondered what you would be like when you become a teenager, when you enter high school, or perhaps when you're just finishing junior high.

I want to see God work in your life in a special way. There are four things I would like to say to you because I think in the 10 years I have worked with high school students, I've learned these are the things that make good sons.

First, R.W., be careful who you select for your friends. Your friends will influence you.

Second, be a giver, not a taker. Much of my job as a youth pastor is behind the scenes. People don't always see my work, and sometimes I take a lot of criticism. But the things that make me the happiest are the things that I give away.

Third, let God in your life. Build times in your life when you must trust God. Get involved in activities which force you to trust Him.

Fourth, help me be a good dad. Talk to me enough so that I listen. Tell me that you love me. Be honest with me.

R.W., your mom and I really love you and we're thrilled about seeing you today for the first time. We waited almost 12 years for you to be here. When we read this letter together 13 years from today, we will still welcome you into our family and will be so grateful that God has given you to us.

Love,

Dad

Obviously, intimacy takes on a whole new perspective when it involves family members. It demands honesty, love, vulnerability, time, and communication. Hopefully, Robanne, R.W., and I will develop that kind of intimacy now and in the future.

INTIMACY WITH THE COMMUNITY

My programs began to build into relationships. I became more global in my programming, wanting students to see that the world was a bigger place than Wheaton. Growing more intimately familiar with worldwide problems could help students' hearts to be broken, resulting in more intimate ways of expressing themselves.

Sidewalk Sunday School became more than a program we ran after school. I spent hours out there building relationships with people who ran the complex and people who were involved in the ministries. One of the things that kept me going in that ministry was my intimacy with the children. It surprised me how easily my heart was taken by some of the children there. Peter, Sam, and Carl were three little boys who needed a father, so I spent time with them, took them to the sports center, and celebrated their birthdays with them. A little girl named Chouck just lay on me and slept because she wanted someone to hold her. It was fun to be part of that loving process.

There are some real benefits to being involved in a large church, such as access to a large budget allowing me to rent a whole camp instead of just a few cabins. It's great to have four or five buses go on a retreat, instead of just one van or carloads of kids. It's exciting to be part of an organization that sees the whole world as its own community.

But there is also a lot of pressure in working at a large church. My program had to be very strong and at the same time, intimate. A student couldn't leave our program and go to a smaller church because, after all, we had the best speakers, retreats, camps, mission trips, vans, and buses. But maybe a student would go to another church because he wanted to be in a small situation where he could dream, where he could be part of what God was doing in a smaller ministry.

The quarterback of the local football team, probably the number-

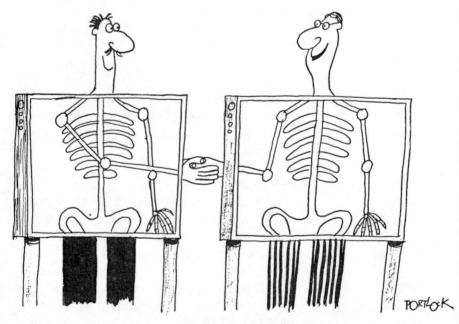

THANKS FOR SHARING WHAT'S REALLY
GOING ON INSIDE YOU.

one student in the school, was part of our youth group until this year when he decided to go to another church. Why? Not because the programs were better, but because that's where his friends went. That's where his relationships were.

When this happened, I was embarrassed at first. Then I was even a little angry at this student for embarrassing me. Finally I said to myself, *Hey, he is more intimate with his other church friends, so he'll probably be more receptive to the ministry at that church.*

Sometimes we get the feeling that *programs* are what draw kids to church, but just having the best programs and top speakers isn't enough. I needed to build relationships. That's why I spent most of my time this year writing kids letters, spending time with them, calling them on the phone, and doing what I could to be involved in their lives.

BUILDING INTIMACY

My first step to building relationships was admitting I needed other people in my life. In 1 Samuel, even David had to admit his need for Jonathan's support. "You will be king over Israel and I will stand right next to you," promised Jonathan (1 Samuel 23:17).

I needed to admit that I needed someone to stand next to me even when I was in charge of programs. I had to get out of the mindset that all students and leaders needed to relate to me. Instead, I could be the facilitator of most of the ministry taking place.

My second step to building relationships was to be willing to share the spotlight with other adult leaders. Barnabas is a good example of this. He was in with the disciples long before Paul came on the scene (Acts 9). However, by Acts 13, Paul had gained popularity and spiritual wisdom so that Luke refers to the two men using Paul's name first. Barnabas was willing to let others outshine him.

In the same way, once students began to feel that I wasn't threatened by my associate staff, they became more open to having relationships with the other adults. When I first came to Wheaton Bible, most students felt that the church cared about them only if I came to visit them. Eventually they felt that if their core group leader called them, they had a relationship with the church.

My third step to building relationships was to make myself teachable. The psalmist says, "As the deer pants for streams of water, so my soul pants for You, O God" (Psalm 42:1). I need to remember that I don't always have the answers.

One of the biggest lessons I learned was taught to me by J.T. Our trip to Ensenada helped me understand that I could learn more about intimacy with God by watching J.T. to see how pliable and open he was to doing God's will. As we spent time together sharing and dreaming, God began to work in my life to help me understand what He wanted me to be and where He wanted me to go. I found new ways to become more pliable in God's hands.

Developing qualities in my life that would attract the kind of friends I wanted was my fourth step in building relationships. When I started to build my staff as a team, I began to realize that what they wanted was my time and commitment. Spending time with them, asking about their ideas instead of giving them mine, I began to develop the qualities of listening, sharing, dreaming, and sympathizing.

The fifth step I took to build relationships was to set aside time. Relationships don't start overnight. For me to have strong relationships with my adult staff, I needed to give up one night a week from 6:30–10:00 P.M. That was a big time commitment, but necessary to developing quality relationships.

A BASIC WORKING PHILOSOPHY FOR HIGH SCHOOL MINISTRY

Every youth pastor needs to develop his own philosophy of youth ministry. Following is the philosophy I developed for my ministry at Wheaton Bible Church. I've found that a written philosophy helps others to better understand why I do things the way I do.

WHAT ARE WE TRYING TO ACCOMPLISH WITH THE HIGH SCHOOL MINISTRIES?

I. *A Changed Life*
   The basic goal of the high school ministries is to give students the opportunity to ask themselves: "Where will I be if I continue on the same course 10 years from now?" Students who ask themselves this question will see that Christ is the answer to a full and fruitful life. At that point, we would like to see a behavioral change and the convictions of students' hearts expressed in their own lifestyles.

II. *An Integrated Life*

Another goal of the high school ministries is to help students integrate the claims and promises of God's Word into their lives. It is our purpose to instruct our students that there is no dichotomy between the secular and the spiritual, that all we do and say is a reflection of our relationship with the Lord Jesus Christ.

III. *A Committed Life*

The third major goal of the high school ministries is to help students commit their lives to being discipled by responsible, more mature brothers and sisters in Christ. We want to see the talents and spiritual gifts that God has given our students be used in creative ways through missions programs, leadership development, and peer group interaction.

The high school ministries are made up of people who have needs. It is our attempt not to fit the students into our programs, but to design programs that individually meet each student where he finds himself. However, while our program may be individualized, we must have a certain standard youth program that allows all students to participate equally.

There are three types of young people who come to our church. The *Visitor* is a student who is inquiring about our church and wondering whether this is where the Lord will lead him. The *Regular Attender* may not be excited by coming to the church, and therefore we need to generate interest in spiritual things. The Regular Attender may need more work on relationships than on theology. *It is a premise of the youth program that students need to be sociologically comfortable before they will be theologically aware.* The *Hard-core Disciple* is a person who is really desiring to serve the Lord with all his heart, soul, and mind. We must provide opportunities that will challenge the Disciple.

To meet the needs of these three types of people, we have devised the following youth program.

Teaching

Our definition of teaching is to communicate in different ways what God's Word says, and how it applies to our lives. We do this through media, music, discussions, verse-by-verse lecture, Bible studies, and other ways that instill God's Word into the students' lives.

Body Life
Part of the standard youth program is to instill in our young people a sense of unity or belonging. When this is achieved, students become a healing body to each other and function truly as the body of Christ.

Worship
For a young person to understand who God is, he must learn how to worship Him. Worship is a response to the proclamation of the holiness of God, so students must learn how to make proper responses. We must give students tools to participate in worship.

Outreach
The standard youth program includes ways for the Student Body to express their faith. We are able to reach out to others through programs such as Project Serve.

OUR STRUCTURE

I. The director of high school ministries is to:
Shepherd the ministry
Pastor the flock
Share the Word

II. The coordinators are to enable the work to be done through:
Communicaton
Missions
Hospitality
Sunday A.M. ministries
Caring
Special events and parents

III. The Students are:
To do the work
To own the program
To share the goals

SYNOPSIS OF THE STUDENT BODY PROGRAM

In sharing how God is helping us to grow toward spiritual maturity, I want to focus on seven areas of our high school ministry.

1. Sunday School

Definition: A time to teach God's Word; to be together as a large group; to worship together; to examine our lives in light of God's Word. Sunday School is a special time for dynamic teaching in various areas of Christian life. Our curriculum is balanced between systematic study of key doctrinal issues, an exploration of different books of the Scriptures, and a topical approach to significant areas of Christian lifestyles relating to high school culture.

When: Sundays, 9:30 to 10:40 A.M.

Key Elements: Music; media; financial stewardship; Bible teaching, verse-by-verse, through a book of the Bible; prayer; fellowship.

Topic: The Bible, book studies, theology, doctrine

Format: 9:30 - Opening with media
9:45 - Time of group sharing with prayer and body life
9:55 - Teaching
10:40 - Dismissed

2. Core Groups

Definition: Core Groups attempt to build a

sociological and friendship base for the entire Student Body. Living out the Christian life on a high school campus can be tough. Sometimes you feel as if you're all alone. Core Groups help us to avoid the "Lone Ranger Syndrome" through inductive Bible study, prayer, and encouraging one another. Our Core Groups are set up so that they can form a basis for a supportive Christian community both at church and at school. It is also important that our Core Groups focus on some solid Bible study. Therefore, we put five or six Student Body members with a mature brother or sister of the same sex where they study assigned topics in order for the students to get a taste of inductive Bible study and *koinonia*. The Core Group leaders are encouraged to share the leadership with the students so students may actually get some hands-on Bible teaching experience.

When: Core Groups meet between 7:00 and 8:30 P.M. Wednesdays at the church. After meeting together, the Core Groups go to various areas of the church to have their individual meetings.

Key Elements: The Word of God; strong relationships built through mature adults in a discipling process. It is also our desire to see evidence of the three major requirements for involvement in Core Groups—accountability, vulnerability, and spontaneity.

Topic: Unified topics are assigned each semester and are either a book of the Bible or a book that helps students read the Bible. Core Group leaders meet on a regular basis to talk over the curriculum and make sure it is relevant to the needs of the students.

Format: Small group inductive Bible study with student participation encouraged.

3. Body Builders
Definition: Students and adults involved in the production of programs for the Student Body. They meet monthly to plan and produce the necessary activities for the Student Body. The Body Builder committees are hospitality, caring, communications, Sunday morning ministries, missions, and special events.

When: The first Sunday night of every month after evening service.

Key Elements: Challenge by the director of high school ministries from the Word and then getting down to planning and executing programs that will meet the needs of the rest of the Student Body.

4. Body Servers
Definition: Body Servers are a group of seniors and Body Builder chairpersons who meet together to discuss and pray for the spiritual growth of our high school family.

When: The third Sunday night of every month after the evening service, 7:30 to 8:30 P.M.

Key Elements: Sharing of needs of the Student Body in prayer.

5. Missions
Definition: Through the ministries of Project Serve, Sidewalk Sunday School, and other outreach opportunities, the Student Body attempts to not only minister to themselves, but to change the world around them. The following are ways that we try to be involved in missions:

Christmas Project Serve—At Christmastime the Student Body will be living in inner-city Chicago where they will be doing some construction, Vacation Bible School, and distribution of food to people in the Humboldt Park area.

Project Serve—Project Serve is a high school missions education project. It is based on Acts 1:8 where God tells us to take the Gospel to Jerusalem, to Samaria, and to the uttermost parts of the earth. We believe that our Jerusalem is inner-city America, Samaria is rural America, and the uttermost parts of the earth relate to foreign missions. Project Serve exists not only to make career missionaries, but also to increase the missions awareness of the entire church body. Each year we take a team of students to rural America and a team of students overseas.

Father and Son Project Serve— During this summer we will produce a Father and Son Project Serve through which students and families will be able to experience missions education together.

Sidewalk Sunday School— Sidewalk Sunday School, a project similar to backyard Bible clubs, is a way for us to express our faith to children in our area. Sidewalk takes place each weekday.

6. Student Body Development

Definition: Student Body is our term for the sociological relationships that take place within the Student Body. It includes the social program, ways that we can encourage one another, and ways that we can help each other grow in the Lord. The following are ways that we develop the sense of our being a body.

Special Events— The Student Body has special events each month. This way we can reach out to the regular attender as well as the visitor and disciple.

The Newspaper— The weekly paper is designed to communicate to all members of the Student Body as well as serving as a tool for visitors to see what the Student Body is all about. We have also designed a special brochure for people who are brand new to the Student Body to help them enter the group. The paper carries lessons from the Student Union and publicizes all coming events.

The Name "Student Body"— One way that we develop a sense of being a body and oneness is to develop a sense of group unity or identity. We have selected the name "Student Body" because we want to be known for two things: 1. We are students who attend high school. 2. We are related to one another in the body of Christ.

7. Parent Involvement

Definition: Three or four times a year we hold parents' meetings that give us a forum to discuss some of the problems unique to student and family life. In these meetings we discuss programs and how we are attempting to enable the families to function in a Christ-like manner. There is always time for questions, answers, and suggestions concerning programs.

When: Approximately once a quarter.

Key Elements: Interaction with the youth pastor; input on biblical parenting as well as some time praying together.

Topic: Family life.

Format: Dependent on topic of the meeting.

SMALL CHURCH SPOTLIGHT ═══════

PAM: Don't you think it's easier to achieve intimacy in a small church ministry rather than a large church ministry?

RIDGE: I think the volunteer or part-time youth worker has a tremendous advantage over me in the area of intimacy. Intimacy is a function of time. The more time you spend with a student, the more vulnerable you (and the student) become.

PAM: Many small church people make the mistake of filling up their time with programs instead of spending time with the students.

RIDGE: Some of the most intimate times I have with kids are when I'm not in charge of a program. The small church person has more time to do that.

PAM: How can I make myself more vulnerable?

RIDGE: By putting yourself in positions where you may not have all the answers. By depending on other people. Mission trips do that for me. I don't speak Spanish, so when we go to Mexico, I have to rely on a student or staff member who can speak the language to interpret for me. To have a weakness and to admit your weakness allows you to be more teachable and intimate in your ministry.

PAM: One of the problems in a small church is that I can become intimate with five of the ten students in my group, but not that close to the other five kids. **How do I handle a situation where I am intimate with only half of my youth group?**

RIDGE: I build other staff leaders who can be more intimate with other students, but I can see where you might not have the human resources. I suppose you have to discipline yourself to either talk face to face with every student, or write notes, or express in some way that you have noticed those five students. My students want me to notice things that are happening to them. If a student's picture is in the newspaper, I'll clip it out and send it to him along with a note that says, "Please autograph and return this for my scrapbook."

PAM: So your job is basically management of your staff?

RIDGE: I equate the role of my core group leaders with the role of a part-time volunteer in your church. The core group leaders must meet with each of their students individually and involve themselves with their students' families, sports, and academic pursuits. My job is something different. In some ways, I'm the senior pastor of the youth ministry. I have 28 associate pastors running around. I minister to the staff and some small groups of students who are working on tasks with me.

EPILOGUE

Youth ministry is the process of God creating characteristics in you that you live out in front of your students. I'm amazed at how much students pick up and mimic from someone they respect. They pick up everything from wearing plaid boxer shorts to driving a pickup truck. They notice how I treat Robanne, how much time I spend with R.W., and what I do with my leisure time. They watch me on trips to see if I really spend time alone with God in the mornings. They check to see if I bring my Bible to church, if I use it during the worship service, if I take notes on the sermon, if I integrate the claims and promises of God's Word in my life. Being a youth pastor, in my case, is a process observed by 200 pairs of eyes every week.

I love being a youth pastor for several reasons. First of all, I love students because they express their love overtly to me. As I talk to youth pastors around the country who are struggling in their ministries, the key question I ask them is, "Are you in love with your students?" If the answer is no, it's usually because the students don't like them. I'm finding more and more that if youth pastors make themselves open to God's Spirit, students will respond in love to them. I can't tell you how much it means to get a doughnut with my paper, a note on my blue pickup truck, flowers on my birthday, or a plaque for my wall—all because students want to encourage me.

Plus, different kids express love in different ways. I've had junior high school students throw snowballs at me or try to drown me in a pool because that's their expression of love for me. But I know even in those acts, they're saying, "We accept you for who you are."

Another reason I love being a youth pastor is because I have the opportunity to be a marker in students' lives. In his book *All Grown Up and No Place to Go: Teenagers in Crisis* (Addison-Wesley Publishing Company), David Elkind states: "The absence of a special place for teenagers in our society is evidenced by the progressive erosion of the 'markers' of their transition status." Elkind goes on to explain that markers are signs of progress that may include pencil lines on a wall that mark a child's progress in height, graduation exercises, or even well-deserved promotions.

I must continually remind myself that adolescents are in a constant state of change. I've seen kids who are hard to love as freshmen, but they become dynamic, spiritual, lovable leaders by the time they are seniors. It gives me great comfort to know that certain students will graduate from my group after four years, and that I don't always have to deal with the problems that they face. But I'm quick to realize that for every student I'm glad to see graduate, there are three more who enter my program at the ninth grade level with similar (and sometimes even more intense) problems. It's exciting to know that I can help students experience individualized ministry that perhaps our society is taking away from them. I can provide a coaching experience for students as they make the transition from childhood to adulthood.

A third reason I love being a youth pastor is that I know students are the answer to changing the world. If we trust students with the kinds of projects that will change their lives, then they in turn can change their world. I honestly believe that if I can help students express their faith, they can lead junior high school students and their younger brothers and sisters to a more vibrant faith in Christ. It may be a cliché, but today's students really *are* the church of tomorrow, and the principles that they learn as high school students will be acted out in their marriages, jobs, and lifestyles.

Finally, I love being a youth pastor because I've seen the benefits of having a broken heart for students. It's been interesting to watch students with great potential be influenced by their peer group to throw away that potential. Or for a student to be manipulated by his girlfriend into scarring experiences. I'm glad that these kinds of experiences hurt me. I don't mean that I feel guilty—because I know students make their own choices—but I'm glad that I care enough to get hurt.

Yesterday, I went over to a local high school and watched the students get on buses to go home. Some students got on the buses with lots of fun, friends, and laughter. Another group of students loaded down with books got on the buses. I also saw students who got on the buses with no friends, and my heart hurt a little bit for them. I thought, *That's who I need to provide a ministry for.*

In *Create in Me*, Pam and I have talked about creating youth ministry in the positive sense. But there is a negative side to youth ministry that I want to touch on briefly. I've learned that I can manufacture just about everything that is required to be a good youth pastor . . . except a clean heart. Only God can produce that. If I have sin in my life, I've reduced my potential. God can't create the ministry in me that He desires. The fact that God is creating in youth pastors ought to be a real mandate against sin in their lives—especially with the implication that the sin in their lives is also being reproduced in their students.

On the other hand, God can create a great ministry out of a clean heart. But you must be willing and able to assume the responsibilities and the sacrifices demanded by leadership. If you accept the mantle of youth ministry when God places it upon you, be reckless and creative about serving God wherever He leads you. Remember, *God can create in you a terrific youth ministry!*

INDEX